Warwickshire County Council

2 0 DEC 2010		
2 2 FEB 2011		
26 ~~G 2011		
2 6 AUG 2011		
0 3 ~~N 2014		
0 5 APR 2014		
1 5 MAY 2018		
8 JUL 2023		

HOMESCHOOLING

0133686355

RUNAWAYS

HOMESCHOOLING

WRITER: **KATHRYN IMMONEN**
ARTIST: **SARA PICHELLI**
COLORIST: **CHRISTINA STRAIN**
LETTERERS: **VC'S AUDRA ELIOPOULOS, JOE SABINO** & **JOE CARAMAGNA**
COVER ART: **DAVID LAFUENTE** & **CHRISTINA STRAIN**
ASSOCIATE EDITOR: **DANIEL KETCHUM**
EDITOR: **NICK LOWE**

"WHAT IF THE RUNAWAYS BECAME THE YOUNG AVENGERS?"
WRITER: **C.B. CEBULSKI**
PENCILER: **PATRICK SPAZIANTE**
INKER: **VICTOR OLAZABA**
COLORISTS: **JOHN RAUCH** WITH **CHRISTINA STRAIN** & **PATRICK SPAZIANTE**
LETTERER: **JEFF POWELL**
ASSISTANT EDITOR: **JORDAN D. WHITE**
ASSOCIATE EDITOR: **CHRIS ALLO**
CONSULTING EDITOR: **MARK PANICCIA**
EDITOR: **JUSTIN GABRIE**

RUNAWAYS CREATED BY **BRIAN K. VAUGHAN** & **ADRIAN ALPHONA**

COLLECTION EDITOR: **JENNIFER GRÜNWALD**
EDITORIAL ASSISTANTS: **JAMES EMMETT** & **JOE HOCHSTEIN**
ASSISTANT EDITORS: **ALEX STARBUCK** & **NELSON RIBEIRO**
EDITOR, SPECIAL PROJECTS: **MARK D. BEAZLEY**
SENIOR EDITOR, SPECIAL PROJECTS: **JEFF YOUNGQUIST**
SENIOR VICE PRESIDENT OF SALES: **DAVID GABRIEL**
EDITOR IN CHIEF: **JOE QUESADA**
PUBLISHER: **DAN BUCKLEY**
EXECUTIVE PRODUCER: **ALAN FINE**

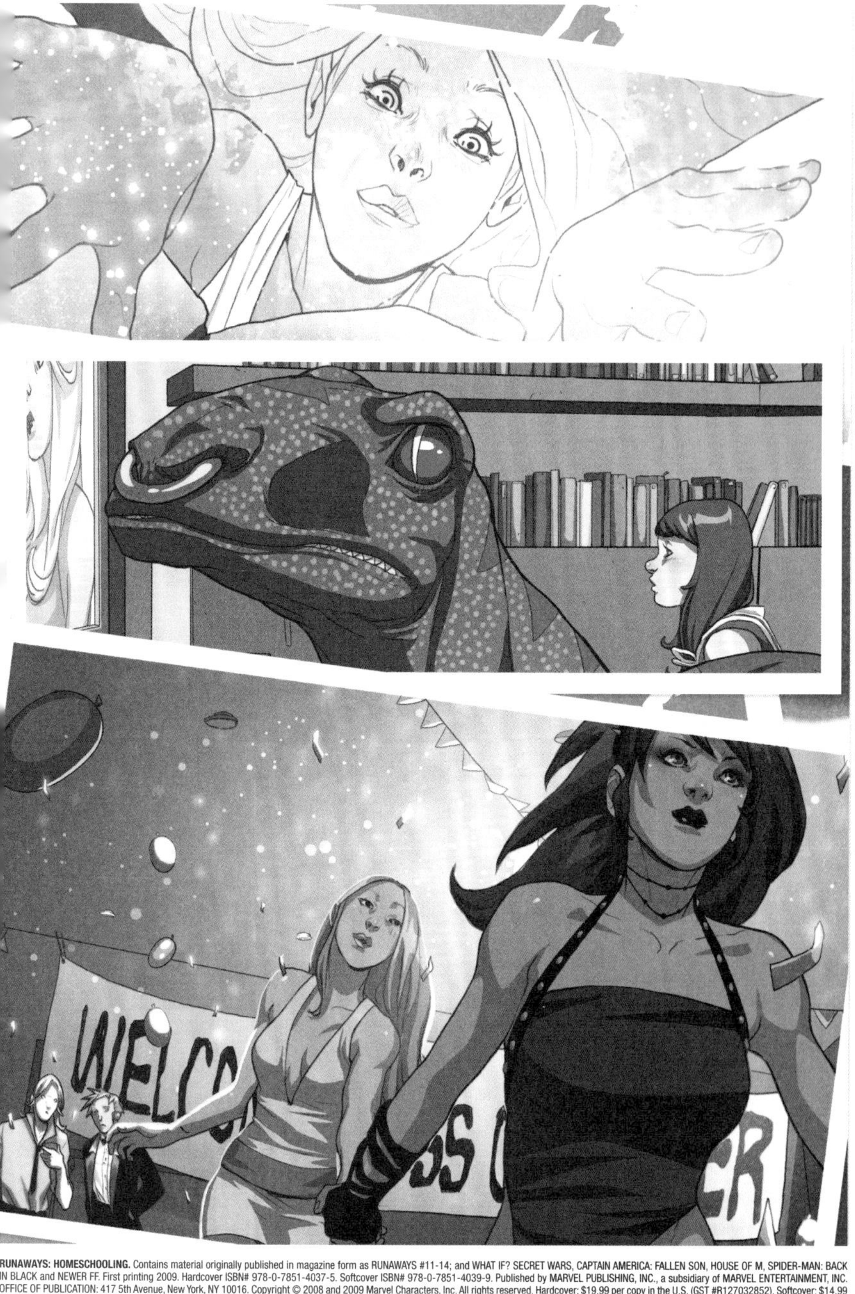

RUNAWAYS: HOMESCHOOLING. Contains material originally published in magazine form as RUNAWAYS #11-14; and WHAT IF? SECRET WARS, CAPTAIN AMERICA: FALLEN SON, HOUSE OF M, SPIDER-MAN: BACK IN BLACK and NEWER FF. First printing 2009. Hardcover ISBN# 978-0-7851-4037-5. Softcover ISBN# 978-0-7851-4039-9. Published by MARVEL PUBLISHING, INC., a subsidiary of MARVEL ENTERTAINMENT, INC. OFFICE OF PUBLICATION: 417 5th Avenue, New York, NY 10016. Hardcover: $19.99 per copy in the U.S. (GST #R127032852). Softcover: $14.99 per copy in the U.S. (GST #R127032852). Canadian Agreement #40668537. **Printed in the U.S.A.** ALAN FINE, EVP - Office Of The Chief Executive Marvel Entertainment, Inc. & CMO Marvel Characters B.V.; DAN BUCKLEY, Chief Executive Officer and Publisher - Print, Animation & Digital Media; JIM SOKOLOWSKI, Chief Operating Officer; DAVID GABRIEL, SVP of Publishing Sales & Circulation; DAVID BOGART, SVP of Business Affairs & Talent Management; MICHAEL PASCIULLO, VP Merchandising & Communications; JIM O'KEEFE, VP of Operations & Logistics; DAN CARR, Executive Director of Publishing Technology; JUSTIN F. GABRIE, Director of Publishing & Editorial Operations; SUSAN CRESPI, Editorial Operations Manager; ALEX MORALES, Publishing Operations Manager; STAN LEE, Chairman Emeritus. For information regarding advertising in Marvel Comics or on Marvel.com, please contact Mitch Dane, Advertising Director, at mdane@marvel.com. For Marvel subscription inquiries, please call 800-217-9158. **Manufactured between 10/5/09 and 11/4/09 (hardcover), and 10/5/09 and 3/10/10 (softcover), by R.R. DONNELLEY, INC., SALEM, VA, USA.**

10 9 8 7 6 5 4 3 2 1

11

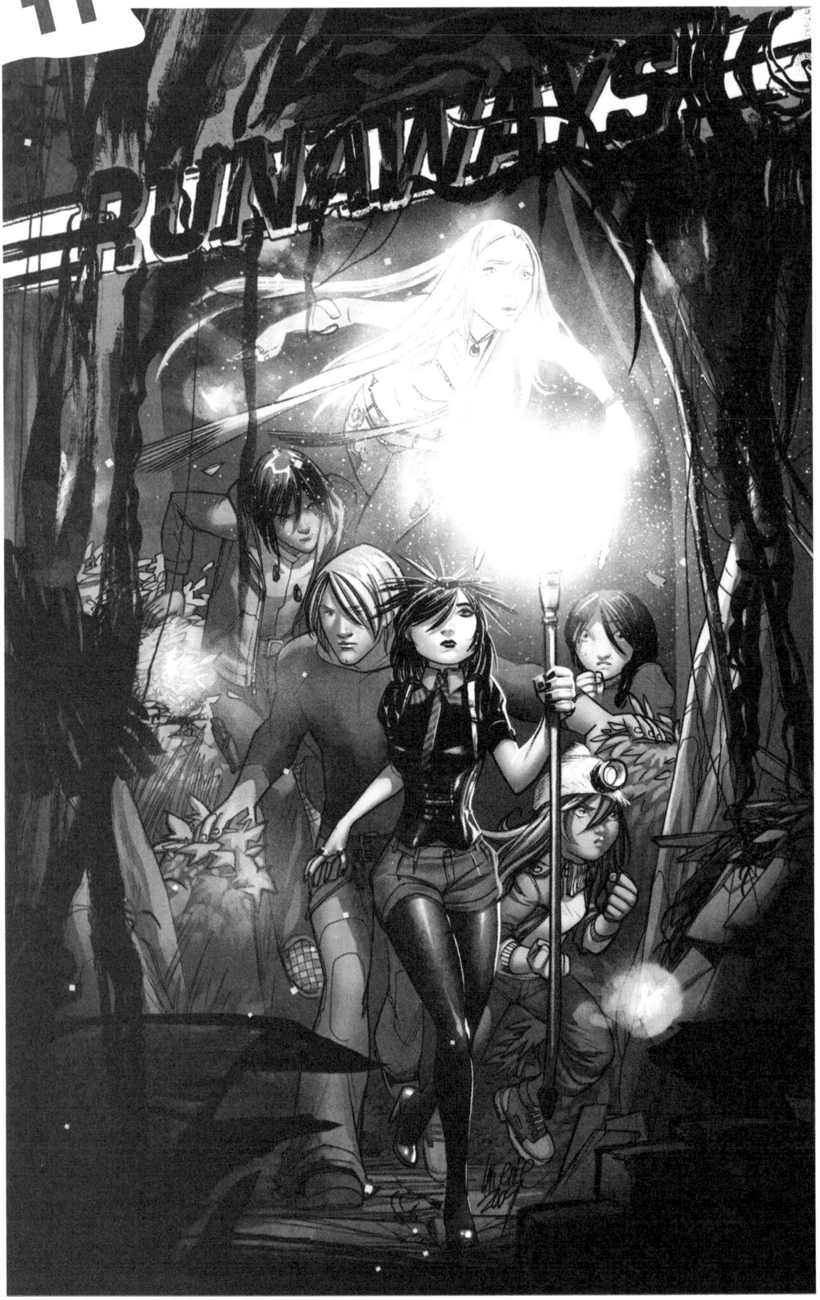
RUNAWAYS

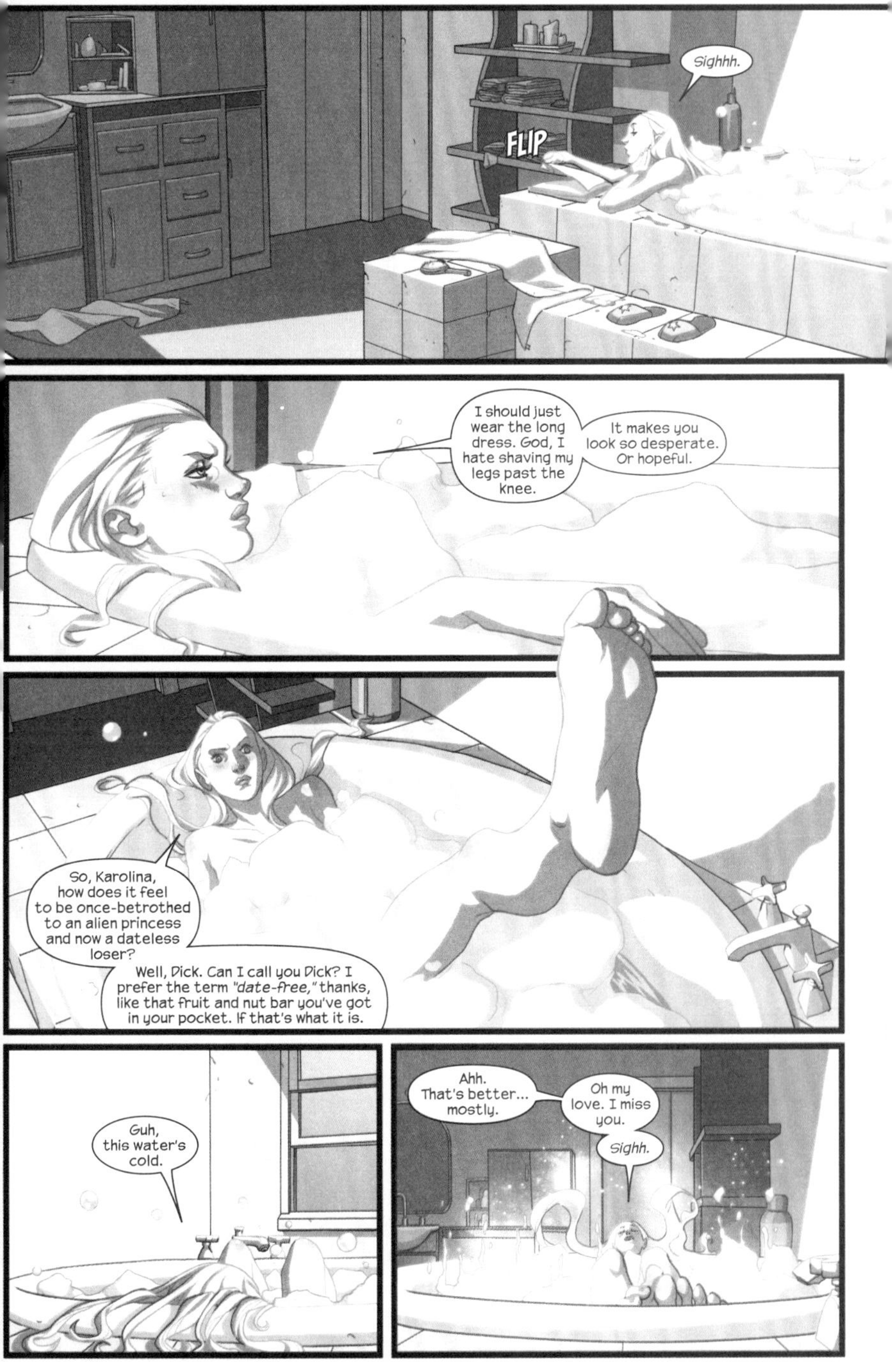
Sighhh.
FLIP
I should just wear the long dress. God, I hate shaving my legs past the knee.
It makes you look so desperate. Or hopeful.
So, Karolina, how does it feel to be once-betrothed to an alien princess and now a dateless loser?
Well, Dick. Can I call you Dick? I prefer the term "date-free," thanks, like that fruit and nut bar you've got in your pocket. If that's what it is.
Guh, this water's cold.
Ahh. That's better... mostly.
Oh my love. I miss you.
Sighh.

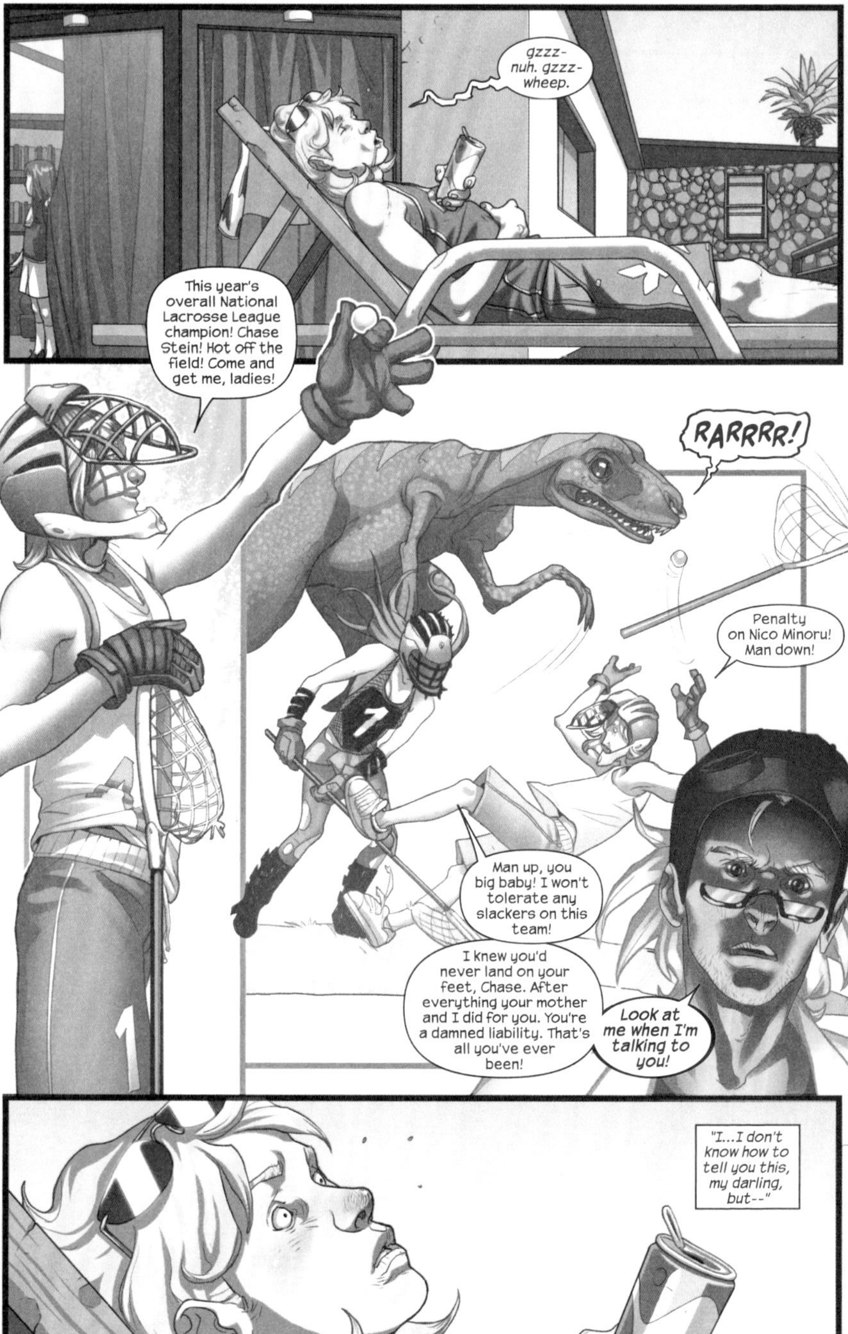
gzzz-
nuh. gzzz-
wheep.
This year's overall National Lacrosse League champion! Chase Stein! Hot off the field! Come and get me, ladies!
RARRRR!
Penalty on Nico Minoru! Man down!
Man up, you big baby! I won't tolerate any slackers on this team!
I knew you'd never land on your feet, Chase. After everything your mother and I did for you. You're a damned liability. That's all you've ever been!
Look at me when I'm talking to you!
"I...I don't know how to tell you this, my darling, but--"

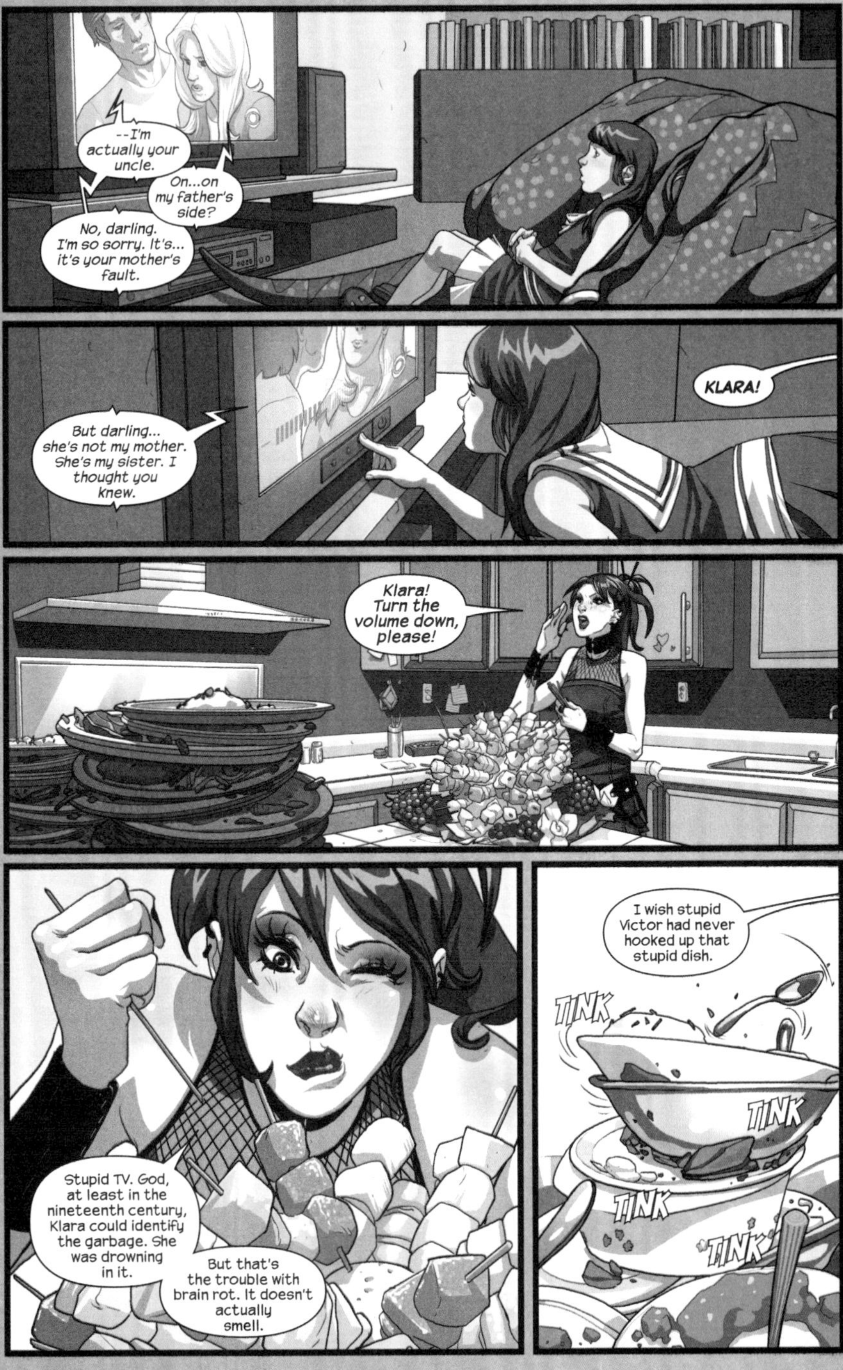
--I'm actually your uncle.
On...on my father's side?
No, darling. I'm so sorry. It's... it's your mother's fault.
But darling... she's not my mother. She's my sister. I thought you knew.
KLARA!
Klara! Turn the volume down, please!
Stupid TV. God, at least in the nineteenth century, Klara could identify the garbage. She was drowning in it.
But that's the trouble with brain rot. It doesn't actually smell.
I wish stupid Victor had never hooked up that stupid dish.
TINK
TINK
TINK
TINK

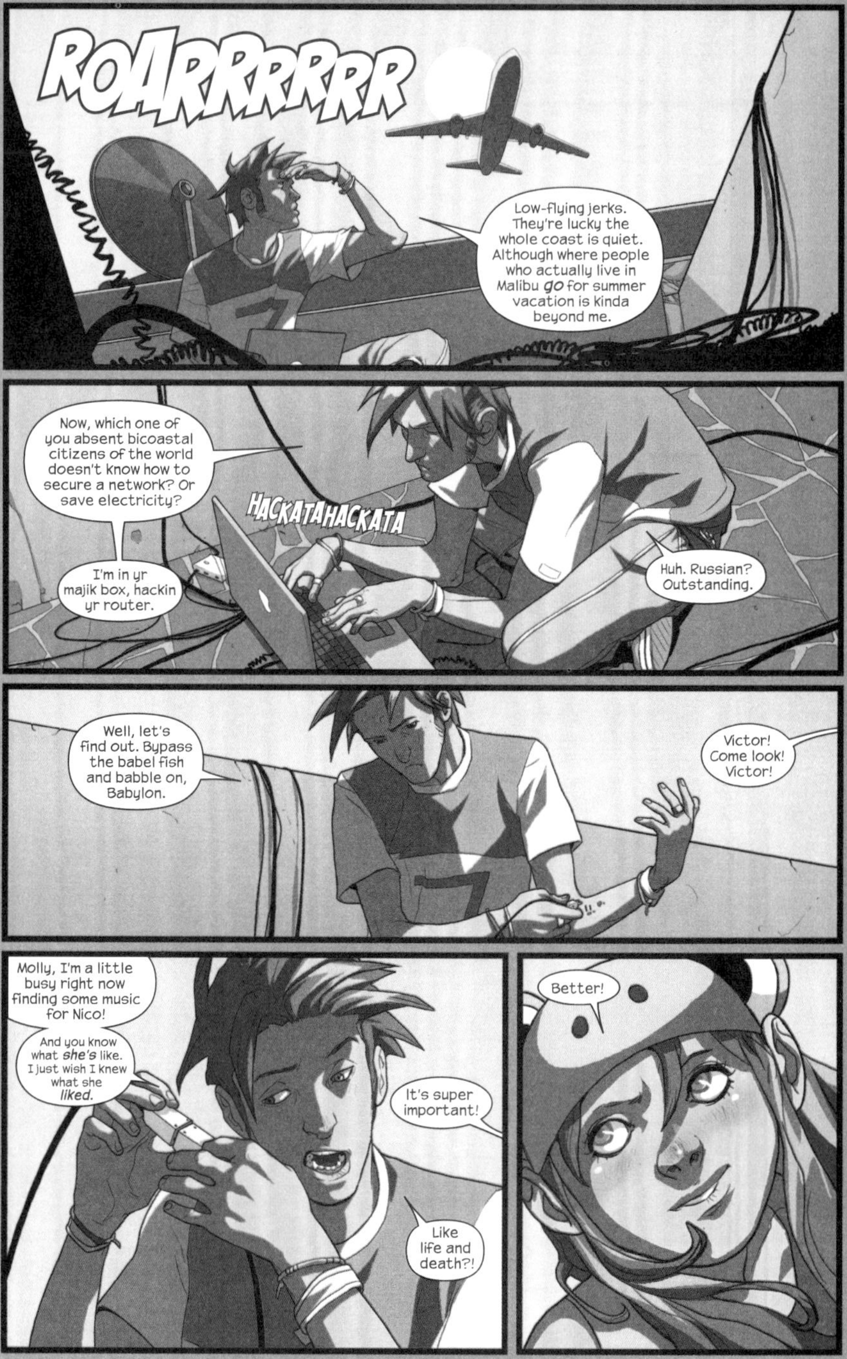
ROARRRRRR
Low-flying jerks. They're lucky the whole coast is quiet. Although where people who actually live in Malibu *go* for summer vacation is kinda beyond me.
Now, which one of you absent bicoastal citizens of the world doesn't know how to secure a network? Or save electricity?
HACKATAHACKATA
I'm in yr majik box, hackin yr router.
Huh. Russian? Outstanding.
Well, let's find out. Bypass the babel fish and babble on, Babylon.
Victor! Come look! Victor!
Molly, I'm a little busy right now finding some music for Nico!
And you know what *she's* like. I just wish I knew what she *liked.*
It's super important!
Like life and death?!
Better!

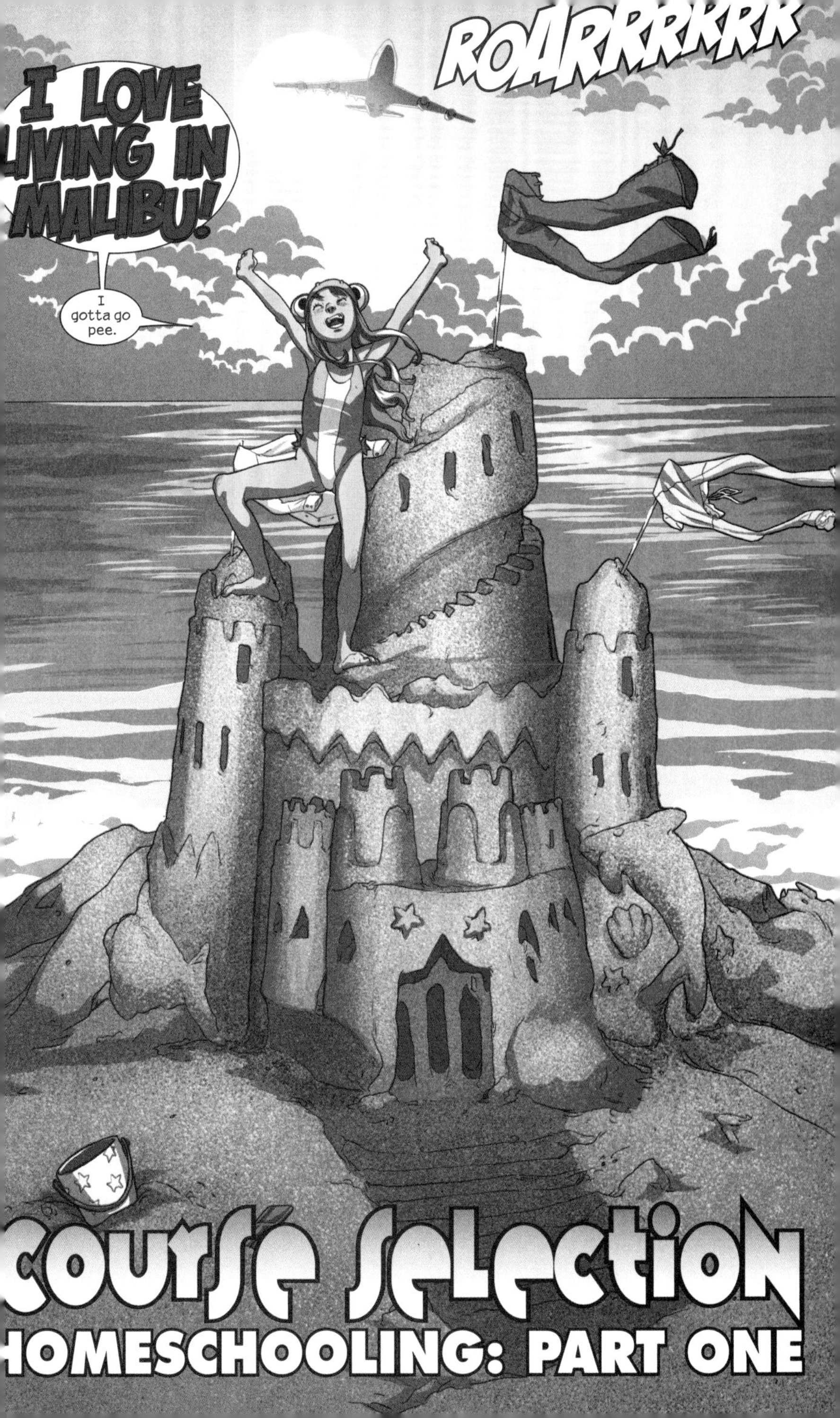
ROARRRKRK
I LOVE LIVING IN MALIBU!
I gotta go pee.
COURSE SELECTION
HOMESCHOOLING: PART ONE

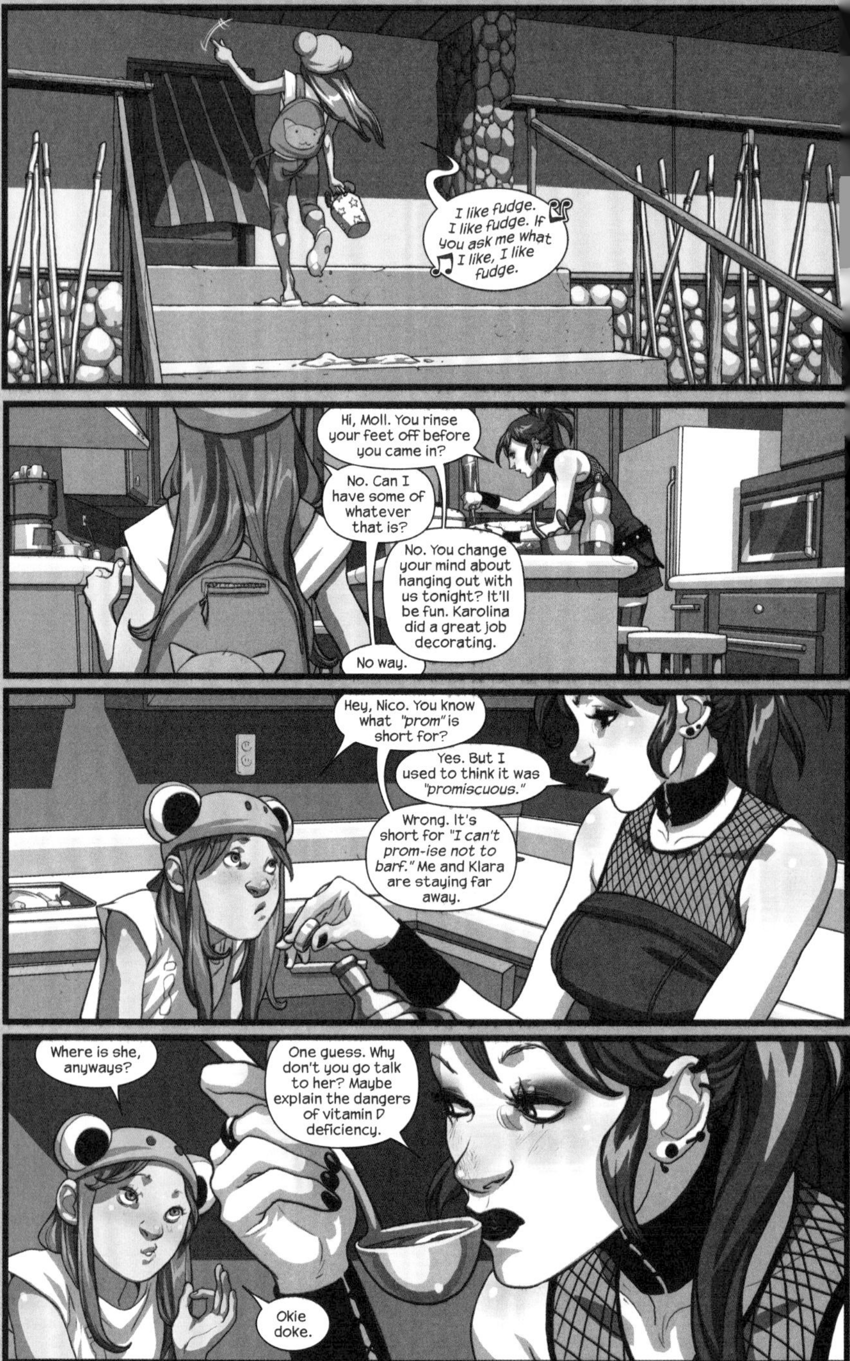

I like fudge. I like fudge. If you ask me what I like, I like fudge.
Hi, Moll. You rinse your feet off before you came in?
No. Can I have some of whatever that is?
No. You change your mind about hanging out with us tonight? It'll be fun. Karolina did a great job decorating.
No way.
Hey, Nico. You know what *"prom"* is short for?
Yes. But I used to think it was *"promiscuous."*
Wrong. It's short for *"I can't prom-ise not to barf."* Me and Klara are staying far away.
Where is she, anyways?
One guess. Why don't you go talk to her? Maybe explain the dangers of vitamin D deficiency.
Okie doke.

Hey, Klaaaraaaa!

Hey, Klara! Nico says you're deficient!

Shhhh...

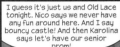

I guess it's just us and Old Lace tonight. Nico says we never have any fun around here. And I say bouncy castle! And then Karolina says let's have our senior prom!

Molly, please...

And I say I thought I never had to do school ever again. Dead parents equals no school. That was the deal!

And Victor gets all faraway-looking. And he's probably thinking about slow dancing. And tongues!

Oh Nico! You're so beautiful. Oh Chase! Smooch smooch smooch.

I don't think it's like that.

Klara, you have no idea what's gone on around here. MWAH! MWAH! SMOOCH!

Neither do you.

Hahahahahaha! I love you, Old Lace! Marry me!

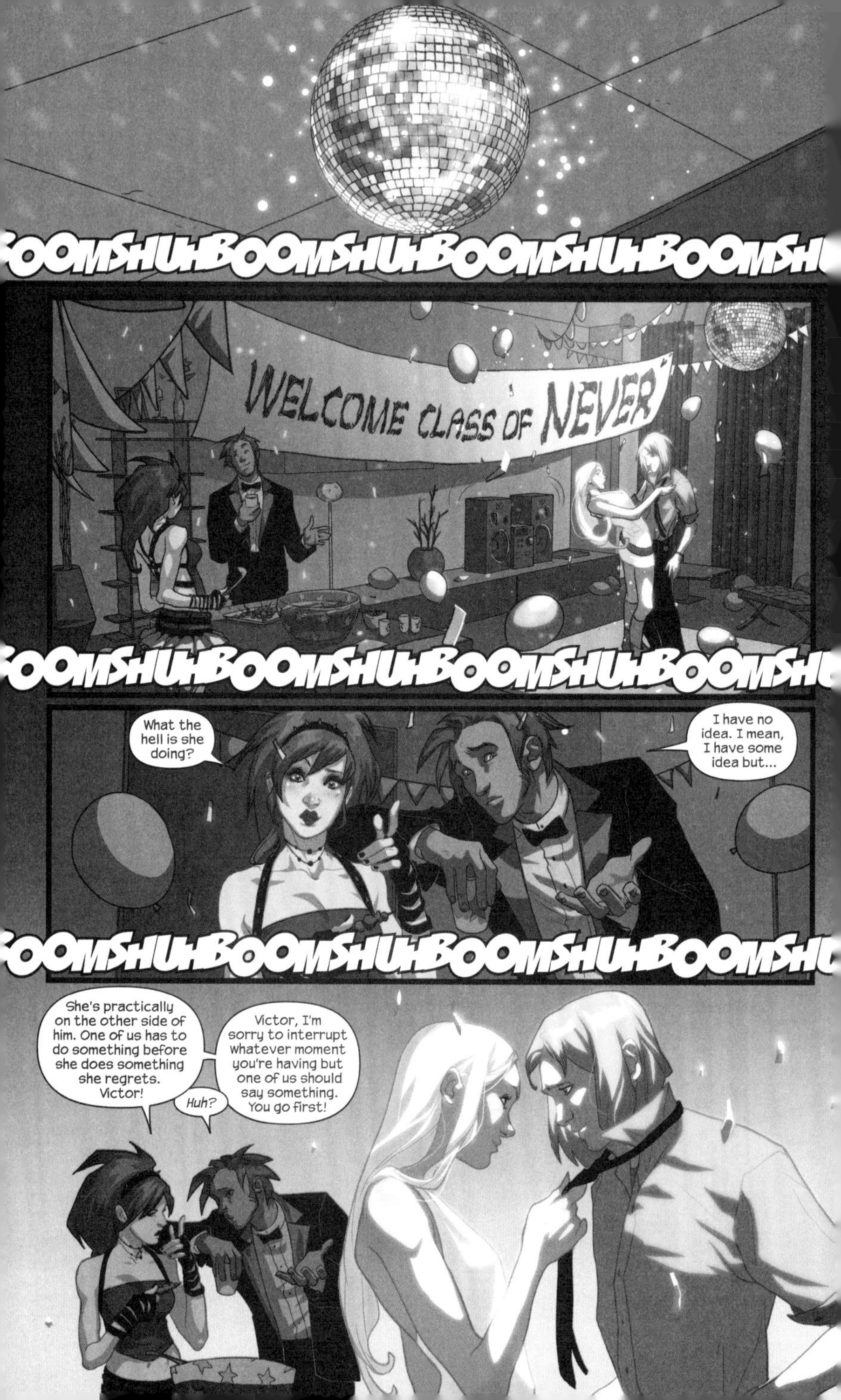
BOOMSHUHBOOMSHUHBOOMSHUHBOOMSHU
WELCOME CLASS OF NEVER
BOOMSHUHBOOMSHUHBOOMSHUHBOOMSHU
What the hell is she doing?
I have no idea. I mean, I have some idea but...
BOOMSHUHBOOMSHUHBOOMSHUHBOOMSHU
She's practically on the other side of him. One of us has to do something before she does something she regrets. Victor!
Huh?
Victor, I'm sorry to interrupt whatever moment you're having but one of us should say something. You go first!

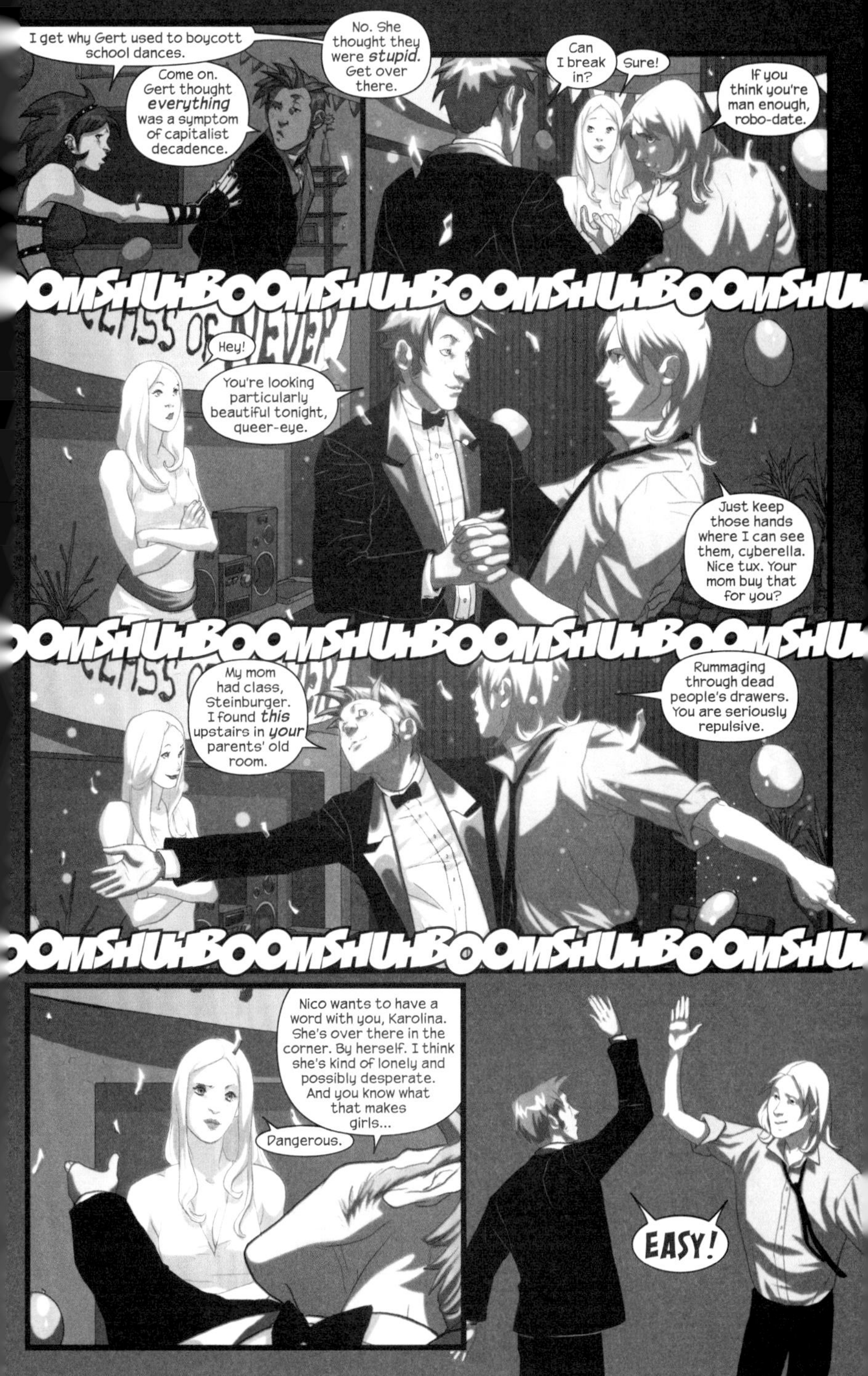

I get why Gert used to boycott school dances.
Come on. Gert thought *everything* was a symptom of capitalist decadence.
No. She thought they were *stupid*. Get over there.
Can I break in?
Sure!
If you think you're man enough, robo-date.
BOOMSHUHBOOMSHUHBOOMSHUHBOOMSHU
CLASS OF NEVER
Hey!
You're looking particularly beautiful tonight, queer-eye.
Just keep those hands where I can see them, cyberella. Nice tux. Your mom buy that for you?
BOOMSHUHBOOMSHUHBOOMSHUHBOOMSHU
My mom had class, Steinburger. I found *this* upstairs in *your* parents' old room.
Rummaging through dead people's drawers. You are seriously repulsive.
BOOMSHUHBOOMSHUHBOOMSHUHBOOMSHU
Nico wants to have a word with you, Karolina. She's over there in the corner. By herself. I think she's kind of lonely and possibly desperate. And you know what that makes girls...
Dangerous.
EASY!

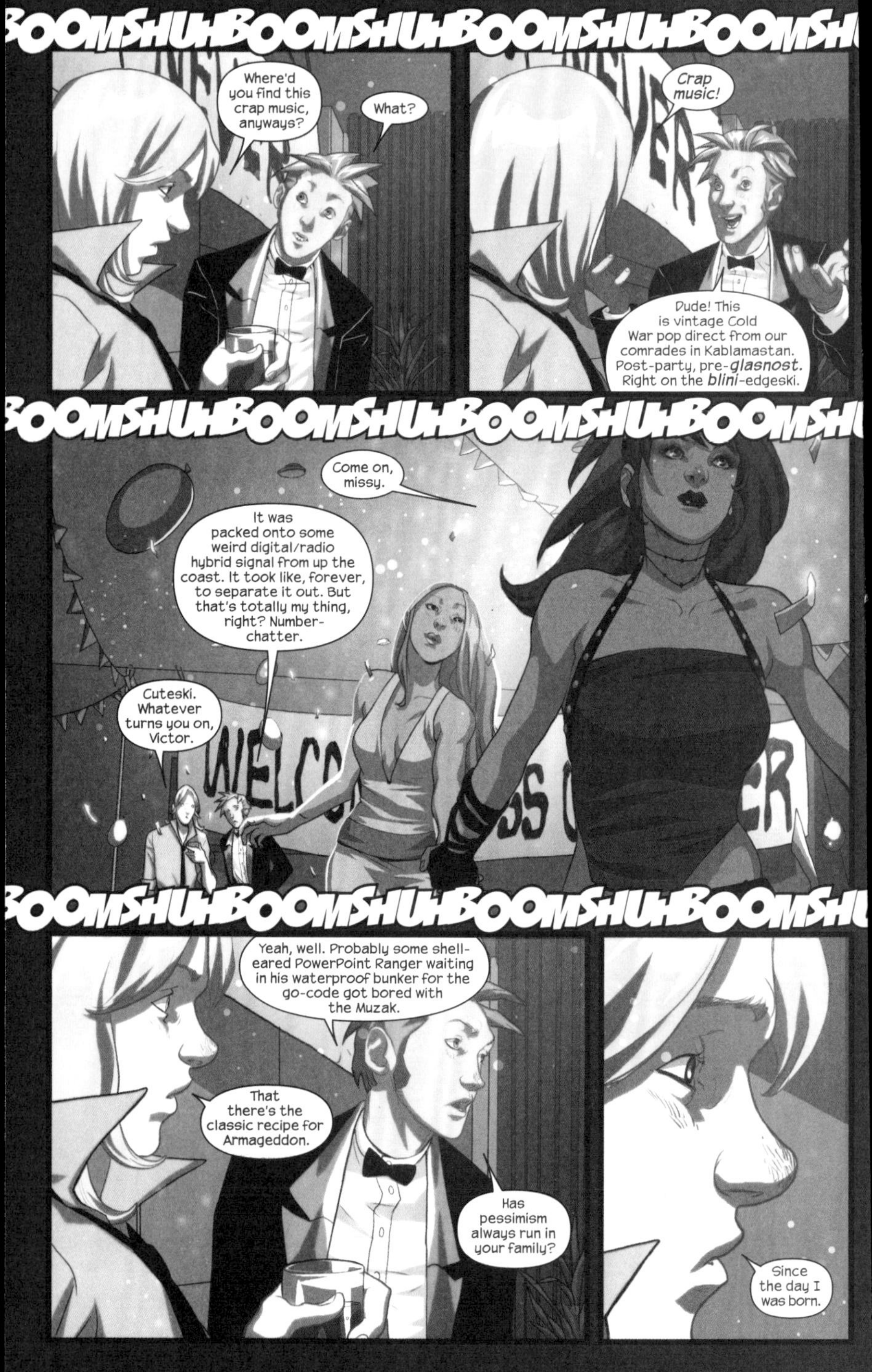
BOOMSHUHBOOMSHUHBOOMSHUHBOOMSHU
Where'd you find this crap music, anyways?
What?
Crap music!
Dude! This is vintage Cold War pop direct from our comrades in Kablamastan. Post-party, pre-*glasnost.* Right on the *blini*-edgeski.
BOOMSHUHBOOMSHUHBOOMSHUHBOOMSHU
Come on, missy.
It was packed onto some weird digital/radio hybrid signal from up the coast. It took like, forever, to separate it out. But that's totally my thing, right? Number-chatter.
Cuteski. Whatever turns you on, Victor.
BOOMSHUHBOOMSHUHBOOMSHUHBOOMSHU
Yeah, well. Probably some shell-eared PowerPoint Ranger waiting in his waterproof bunker for the go-code got bored with the Muzak.
That there's the classic recipe for Armageddon.
Has pessimism always run in your family?
Since the day I was born.

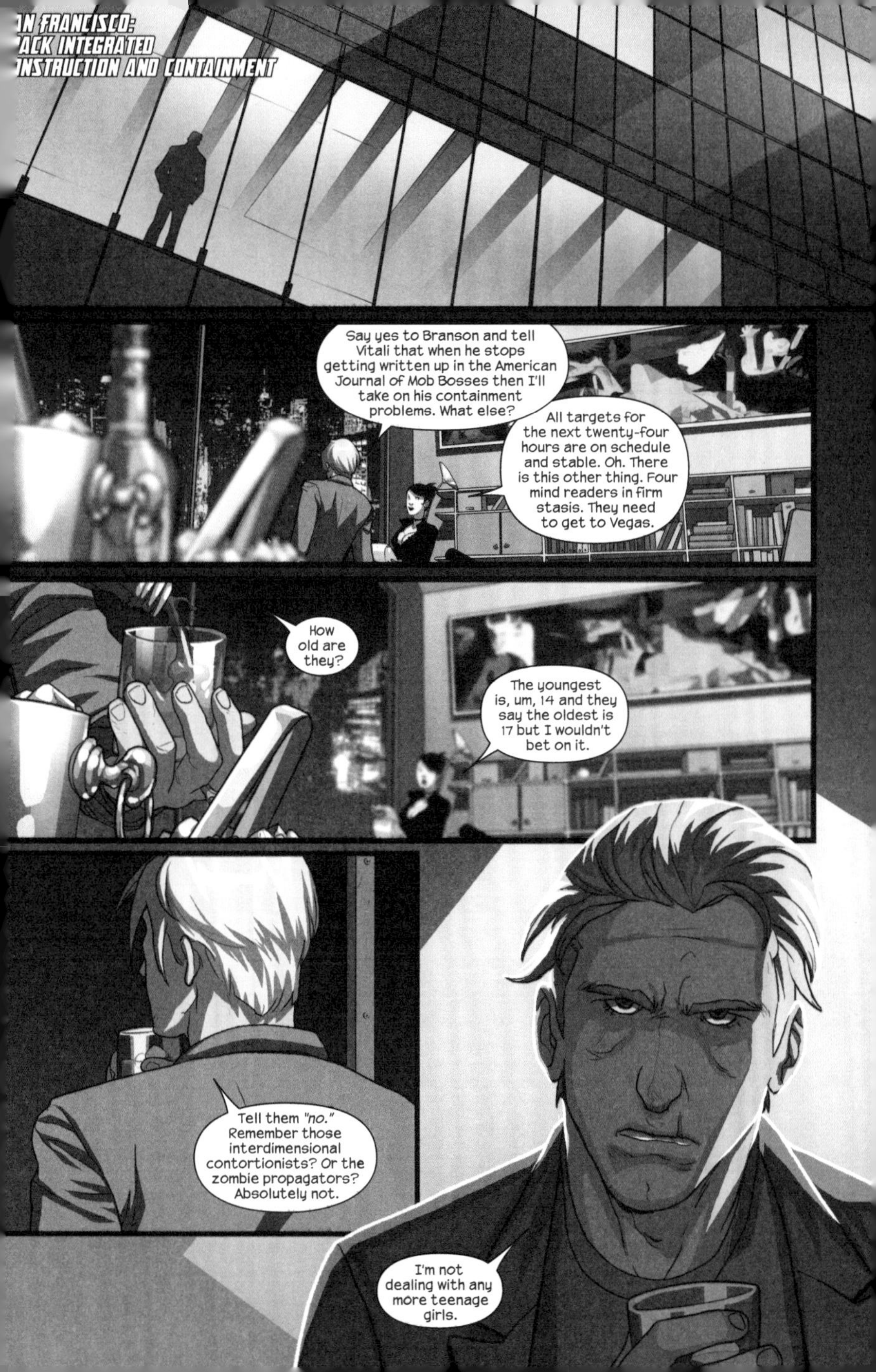
AN FRANCISCO:
ACK INTEGRATED
NSTRUCTION AND CONTAINMENT
Say yes to Branson and tell Vitali that when he stops getting written up in the American Journal of Mob Bosses then I'll take on his containment problems. What else?
All targets for the next twenty-four hours are on schedule and stable. Oh. There is this other thing. Four mind readers in firm stasis. They need to get to Vegas.
How old are they?
The youngest is, um, 14 and they say the oldest is 17 but I wouldn't bet on it.
Tell them *"no."* Remember those interdimensional contortionists? Or the zombie propagators? Absolutely not.
I'm not dealing with any more teenage girls.

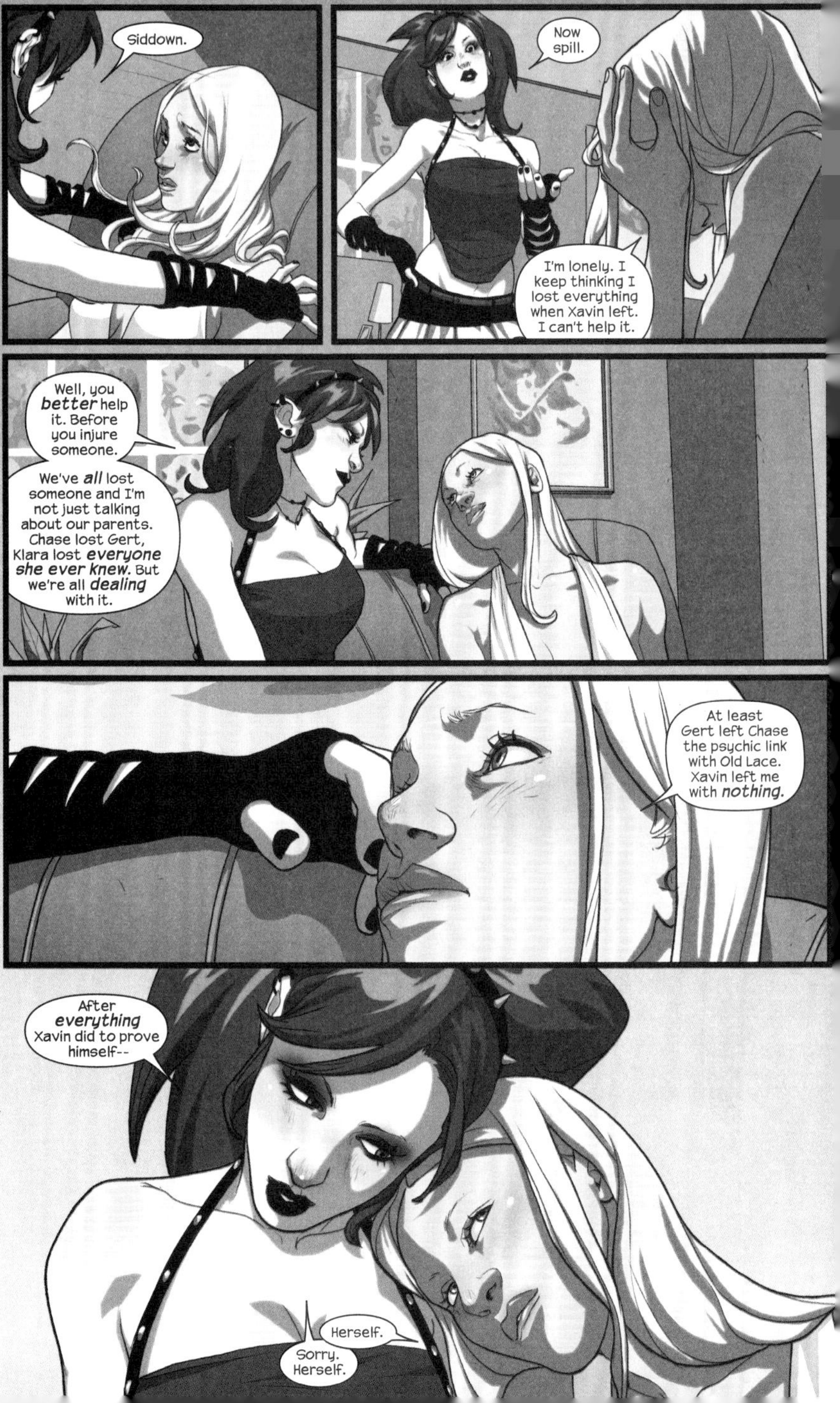
Siddown.
Now spill.
I'm lonely. I keep thinking I lost everything when Xavin left. I can't help it.
Well, you better help it. Before you injure someone.
We've all lost someone and I'm not just talking about our parents. Chase lost Gert, Klara lost everyone she ever knew. But we're all dealing with it.
At least Gert left Chase the psychic link with Old Lace. Xavin left me with nothing.
After everything Xavin did to prove himself--
Herself.
Sorry. Herself.

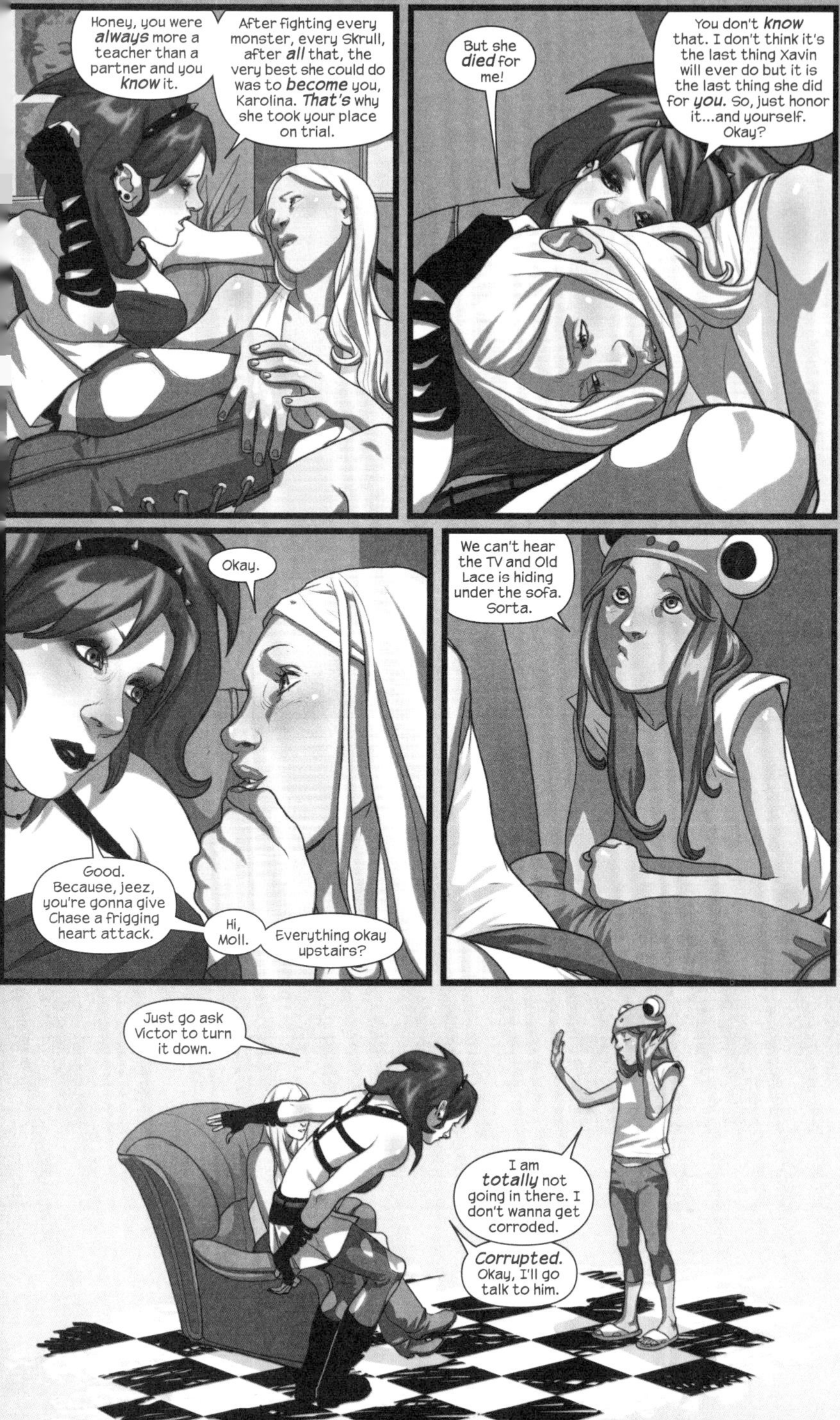

Honey, you were *always* more a teacher than a partner and you *know* it.
After fighting every monster, every Skrull, after *all* that, the very best she could do was to *become* you, Karolina. *That's* why she took your place on trial.
But she *died* for me!
You don't *know* that. I don't think it's the last thing Xavin will ever do but it is the last thing she did for *you*. So, just honor it...and yourself. Okay?
Okay.
Good. Because, jeez, you're gonna give Chase a frigging heart attack.
Hi, Moll.
Everything okay upstairs?
We can't hear the TV and Old Lace is hiding under the sofa. Sorta.
Just go ask Victor to turn it down.
I am *totally* not going in there. I don't wanna get corroded.
Corrupted. Okay, I'll go talk to him.

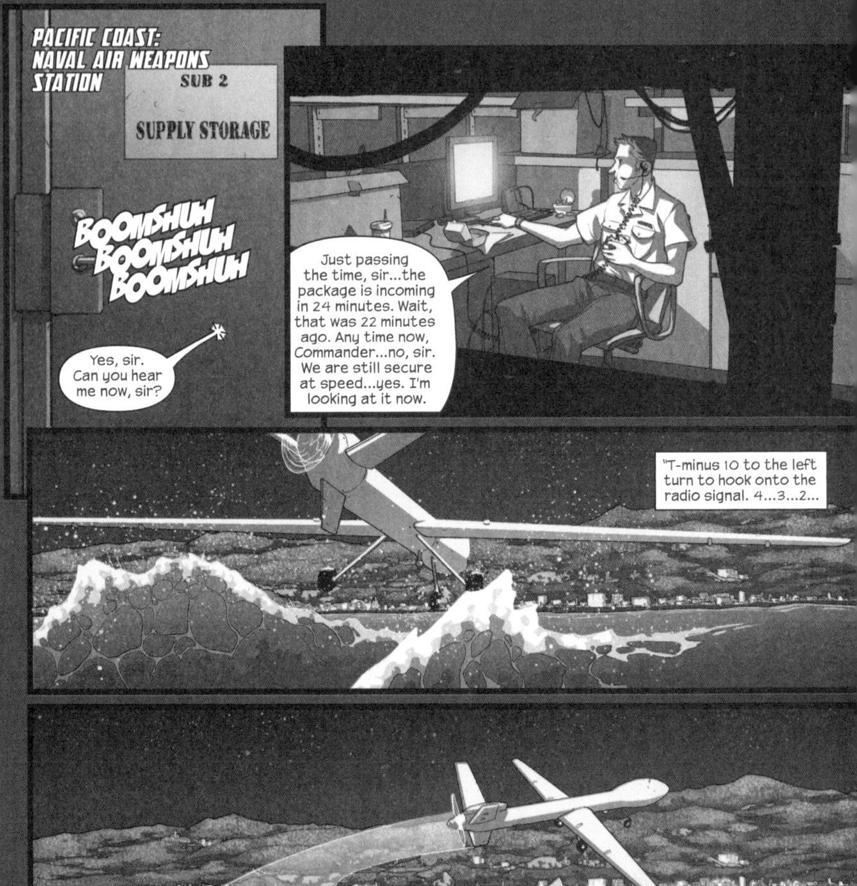

PACIFIC COAST: NAVAL AIR WEAPONS STATION
SUB 2
SUPPLY STORAGE
BOOMSHUH BOOMSHUH BOOMSHUH
Just passing the time, sir...the package is incoming in 24 minutes. Wait, that was 22 minutes ago. Any time now, Commander...no, sir. We are still secure at speed...yes. I'm looking at it now.
Yes, sir. Can you hear me now, sir?
"T-minus 10 to the left turn to hook onto the radio signal. 4...3...2...
"Oh Shiatsu."
Mrrh?
Now there's no excuse for laziness. This new device does all the work for you. Call now!

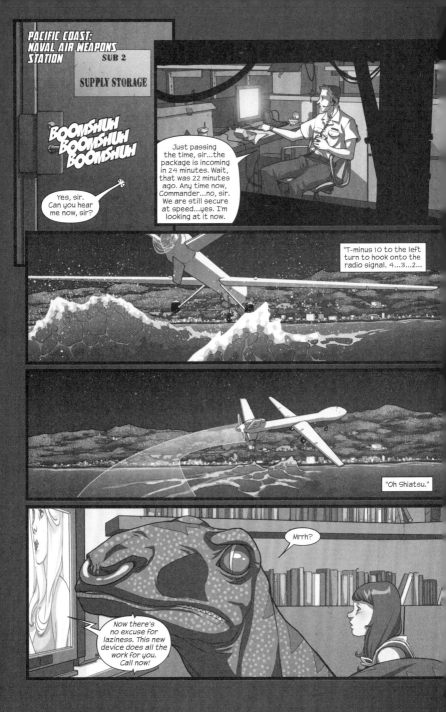

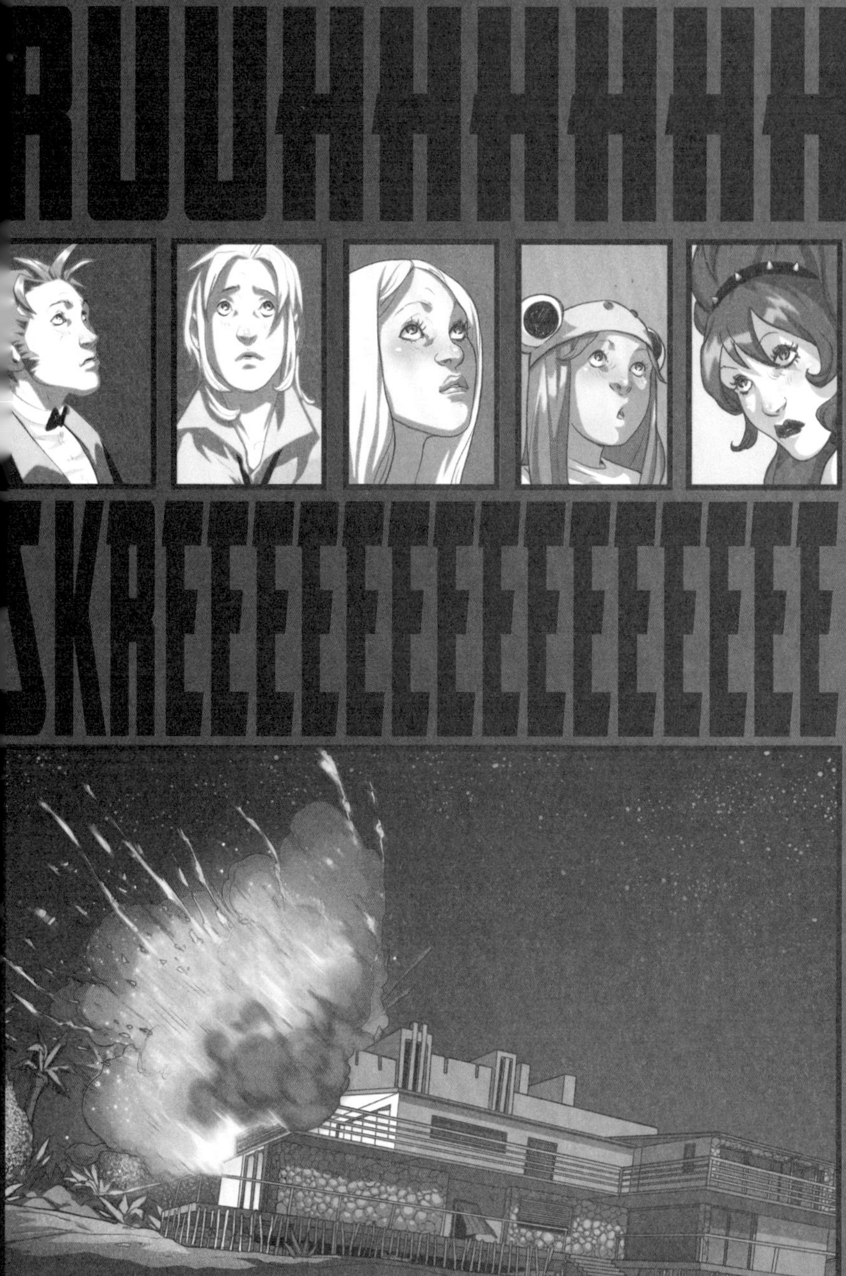
RUUHHHHHHH
SKREEEEEEEEEEEEEEEE

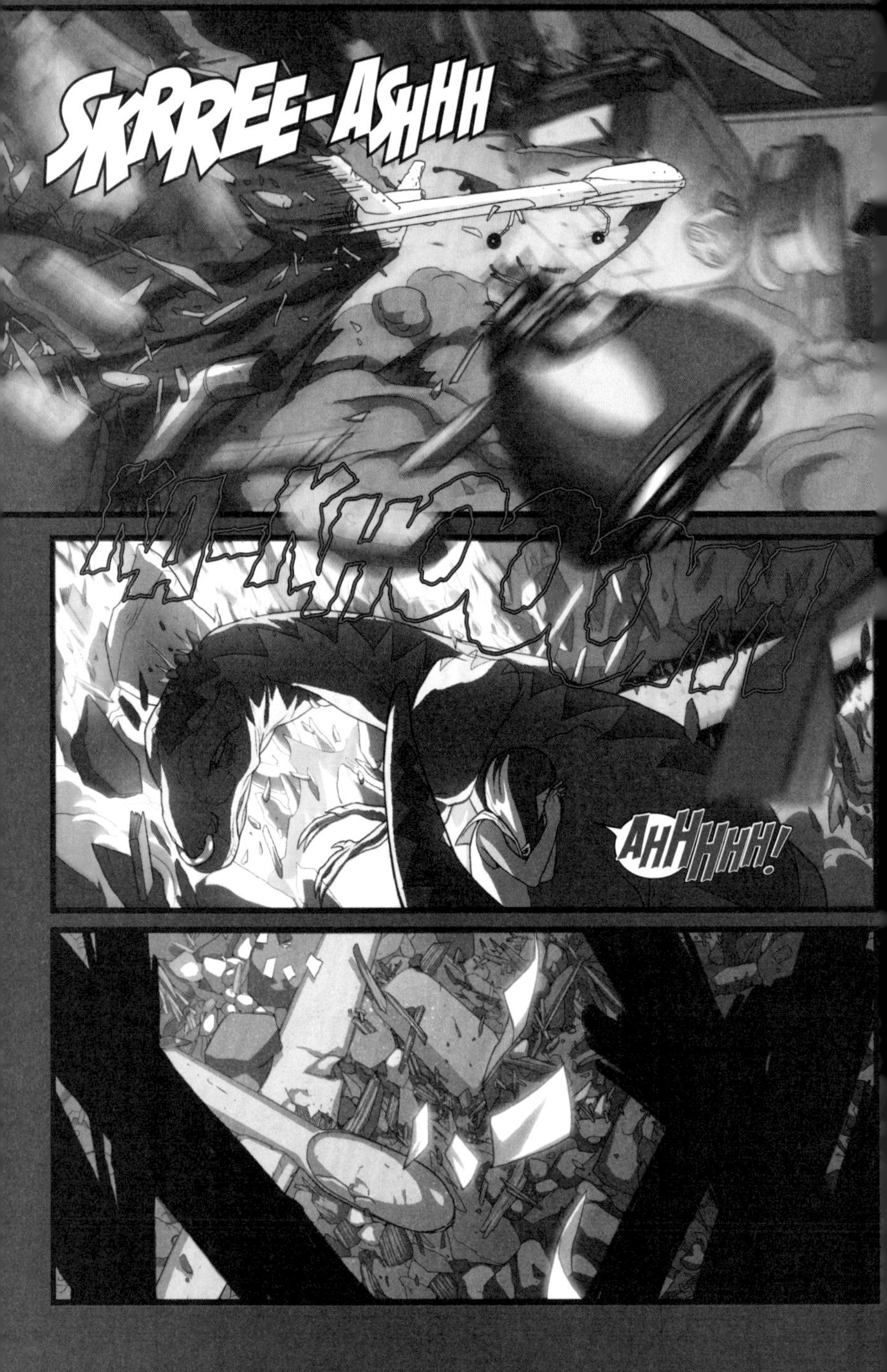
SKRREE-ASHHH
KA-WHOOOM
AHHHHH!

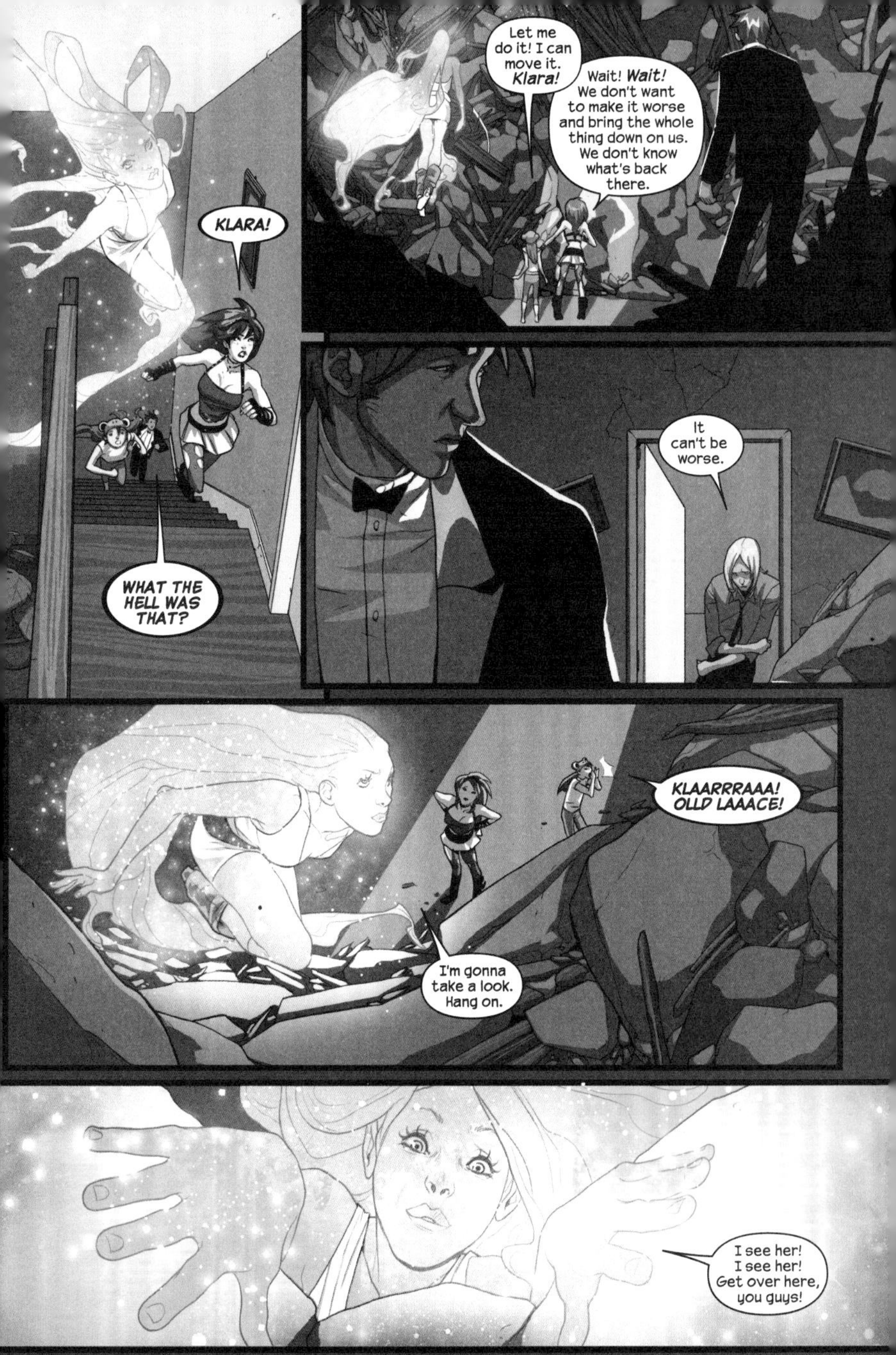
KLARA!
WHAT THE HELL WAS THAT?
Let me do it! I can move it. Klara!
Wait! Wait! We don't want to make it worse and bring the whole thing down on us. We don't know what's back there.
It can't be worse.
KLAARRRAAA! OLLD LAAACE!
I'm gonna take a look. Hang on.
I see her! I see her! Get over here, you guys!

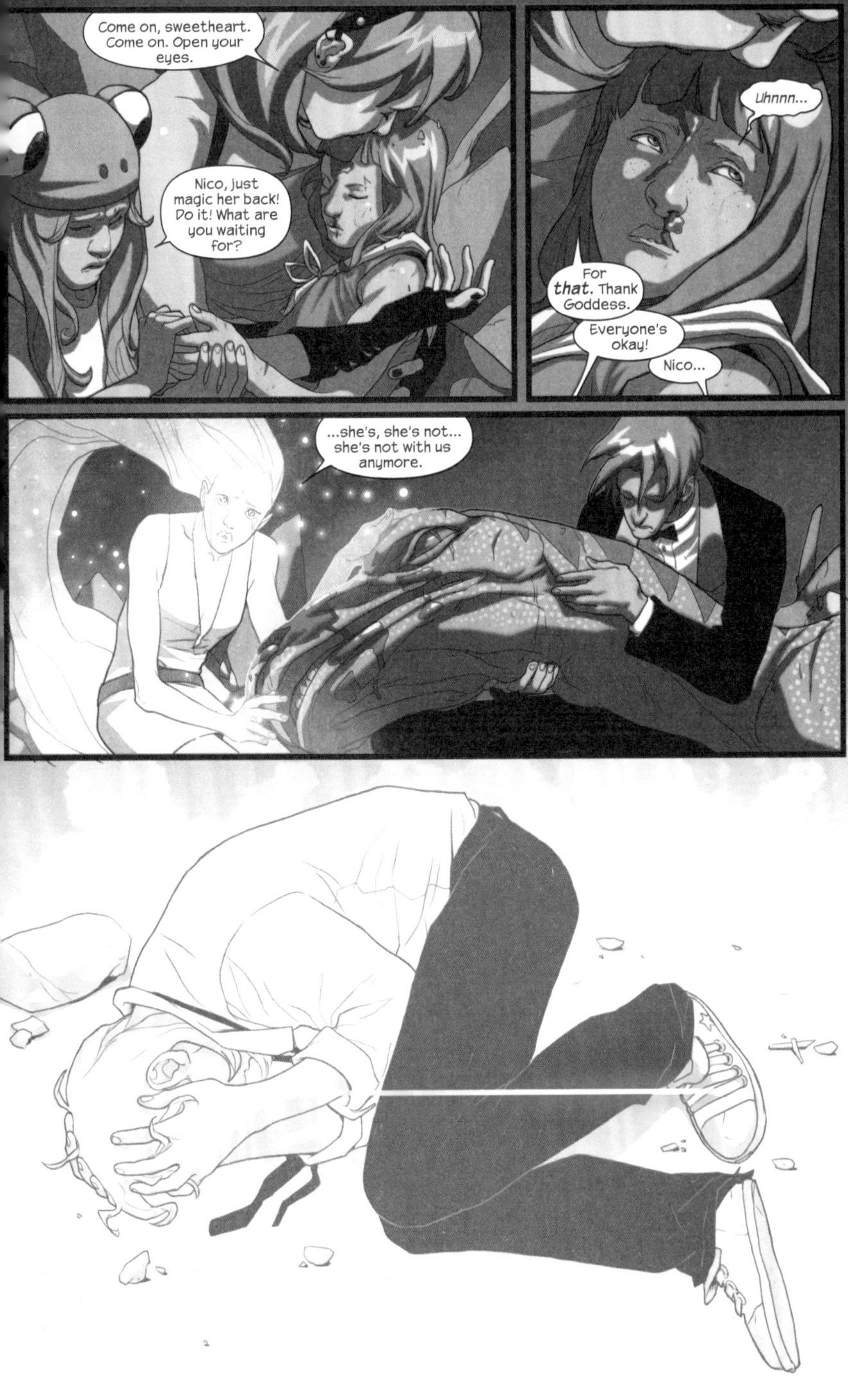
Come on, sweetheart. Come on. Open your eyes.
Nico, just magic her back! Do it! What are you waiting for?
Uhnnn...
For *that.* Thank Goddess.
Everyone's okay!
Nico...
...she's, she's not... she's not with us anymore.

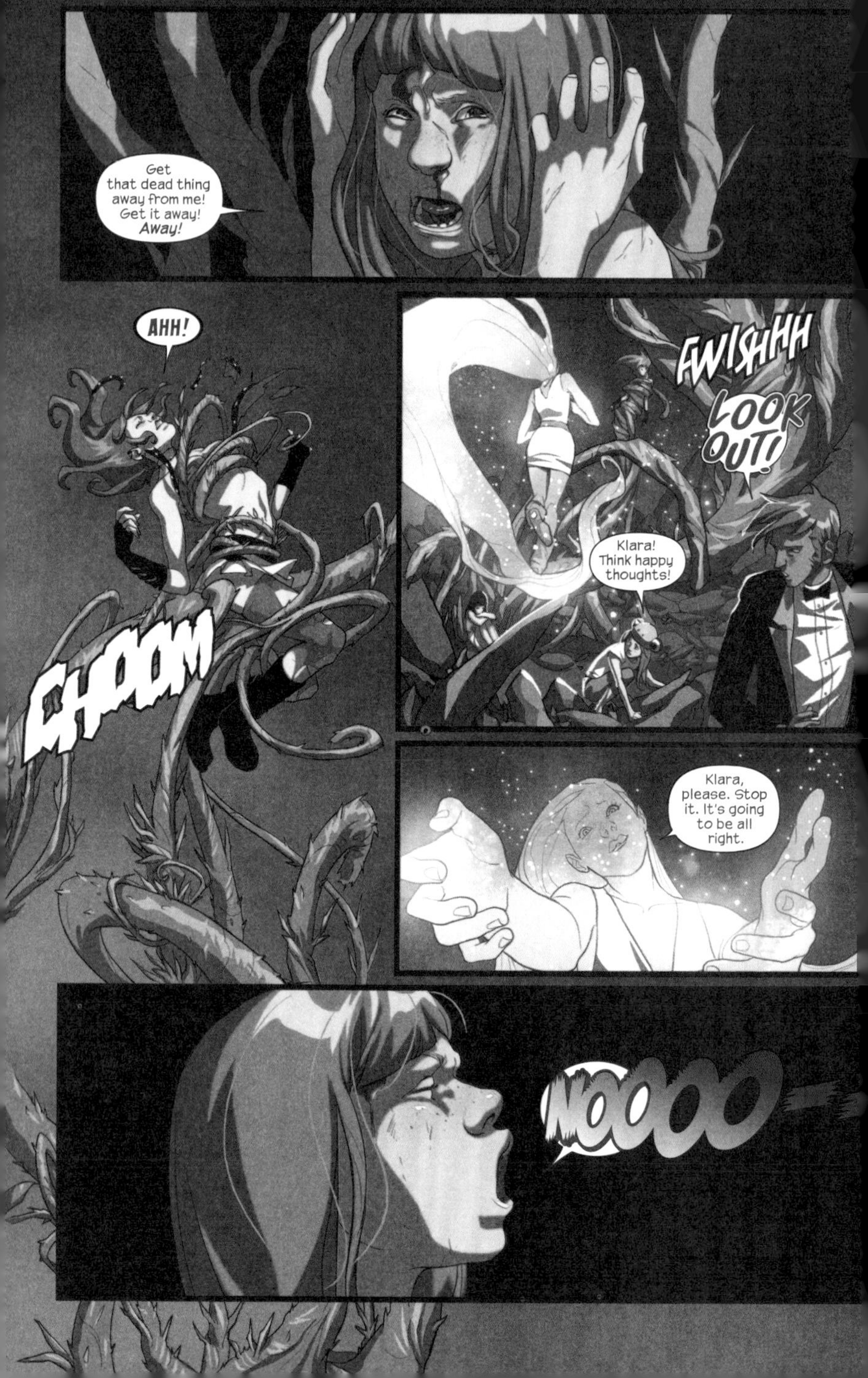

Get that dead thing away from me! Get it away! *Away!*
AHH!
CHOOM
FWISHHH
LOOK OUT!
Klara! Think happy thoughts!
Klara, please. Stop it. It's going to be all right.
NOOOO

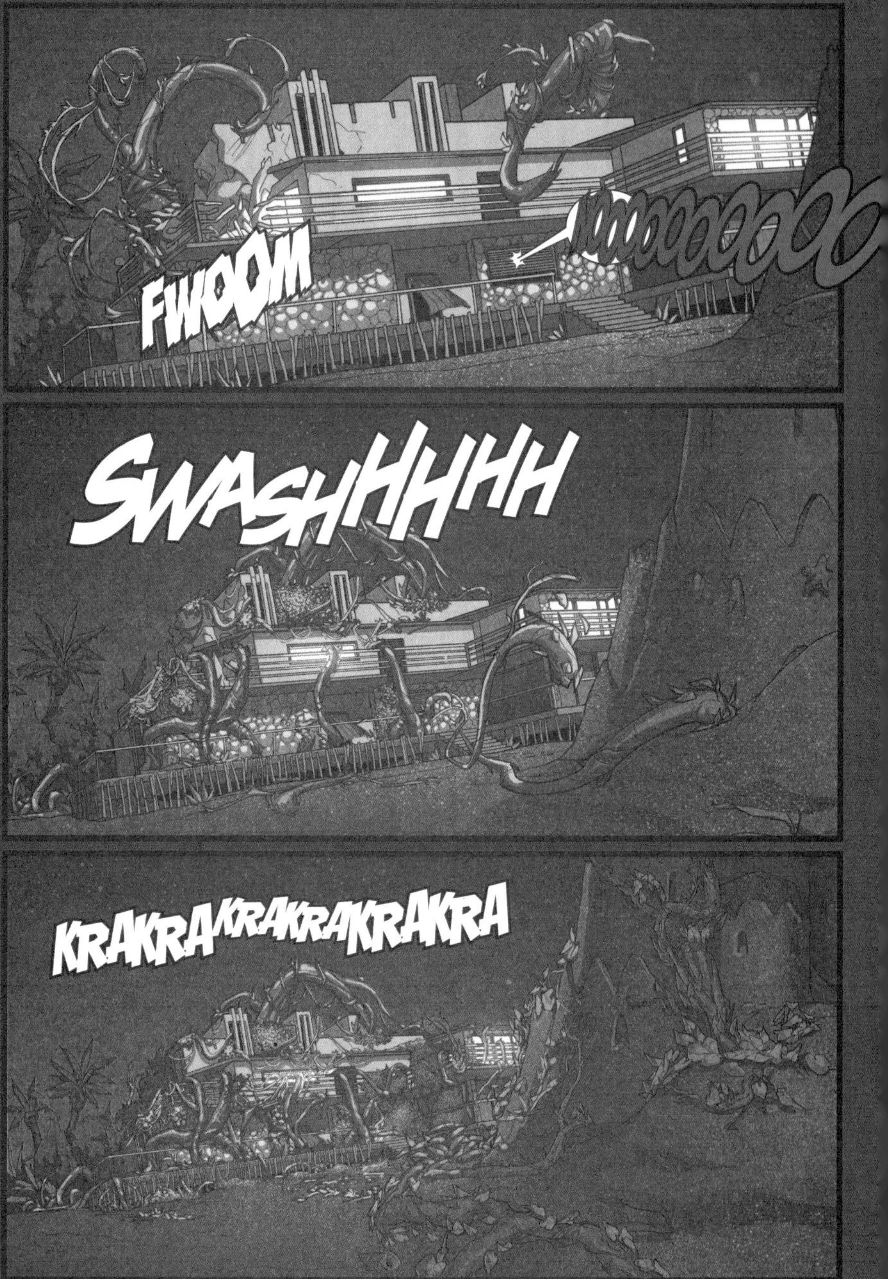
FWOOM
NOOOOOOOOOOOO
SWASHHHHH
KRAKRAKRAKRAKRAKRA

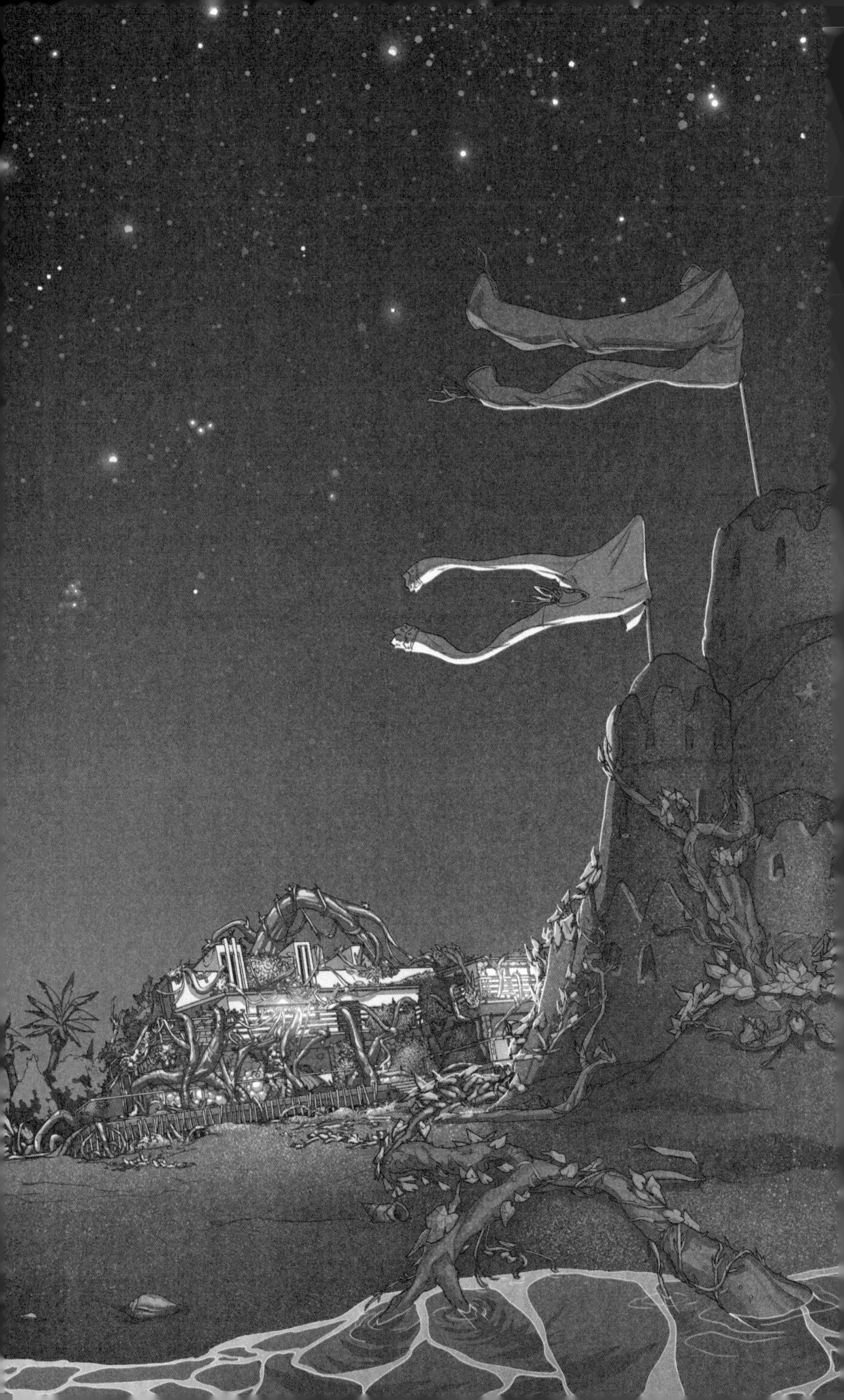

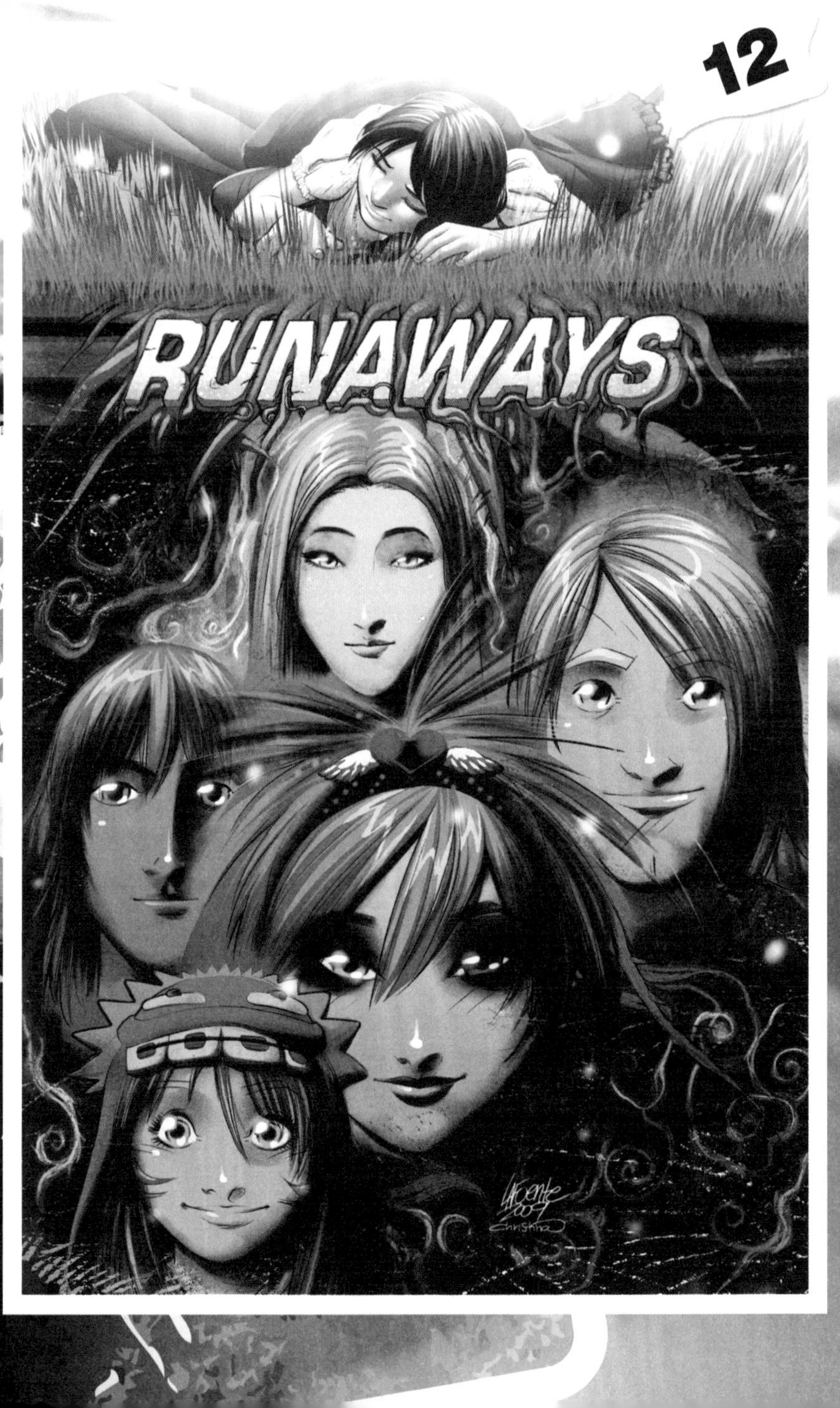
12
RUNAWAYS
LaFuente 2007
Christina

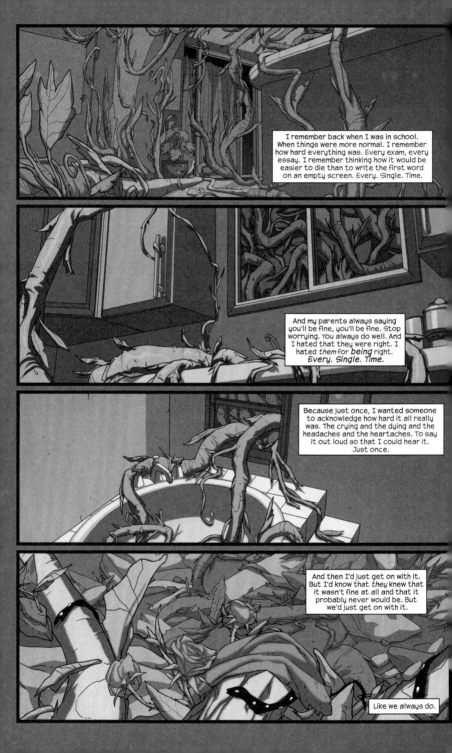

I remember back when I was in school. When things were more normal. I remember how hard everything was. Every exam, every essay. I remember thinking how it would be easier to die than to write the first word on an empty screen. Every. Single. Time.

And my parents always saying you'll be fine, you'll be fine. Stop worrying. You always do well. And I hated that they were right. I hated *them* for *being* right. *Every. Single. Time.*

Because just once, I wanted someone to acknowledge how hard it all really was. The crying and the dying and the headaches and the heartaches. To say it out loud so that I could hear it. Just once.

And then I'd just get on with it. But I'd know that *they* knew that it wasn't fine at all and that it probably never would be. But we'd just get on with it.

Like we always do.

HOMESCHOOLING: PART TWO

FUNCTIONS AND RELATIONS

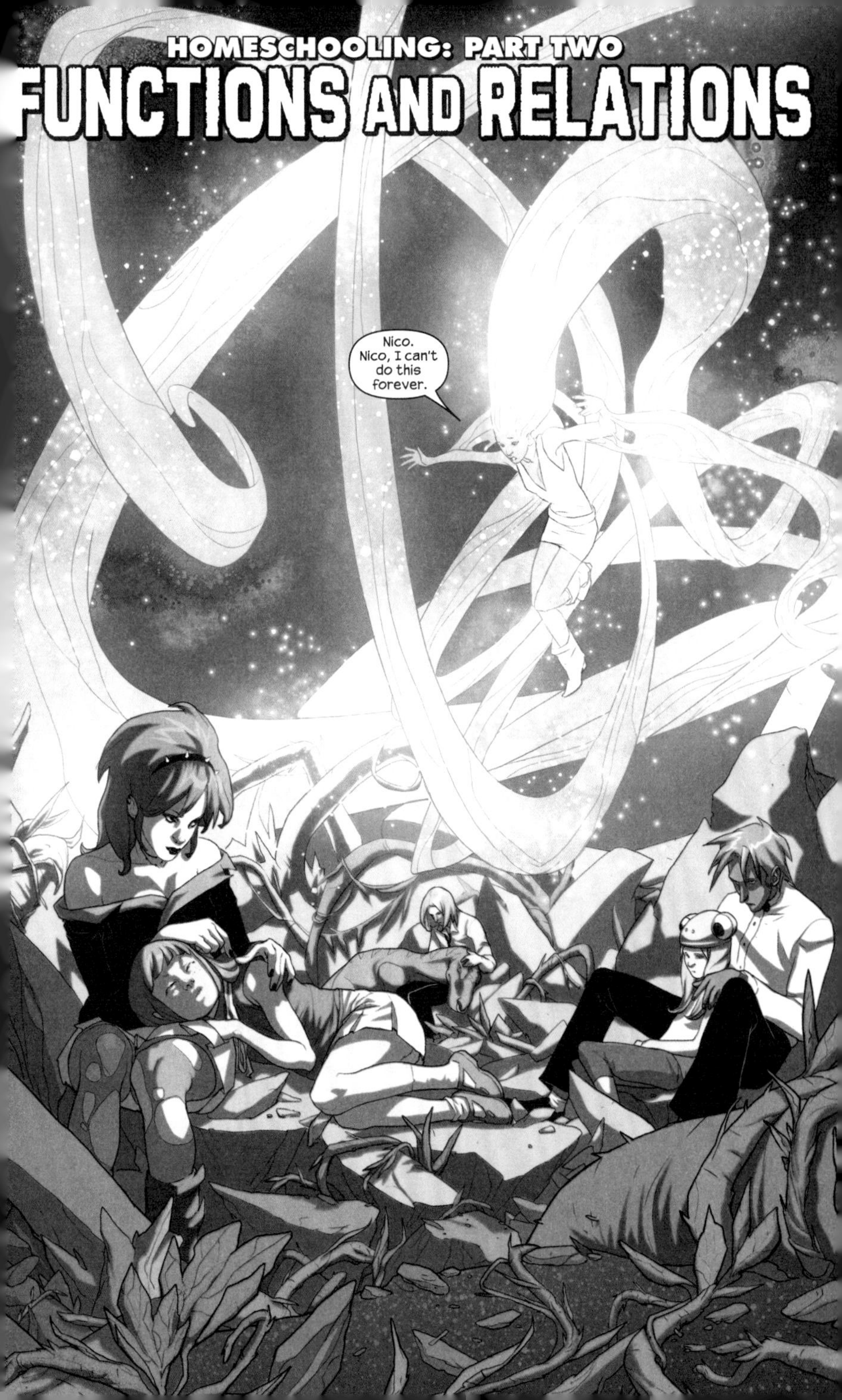

Nico. Nico, I can't do this forever.

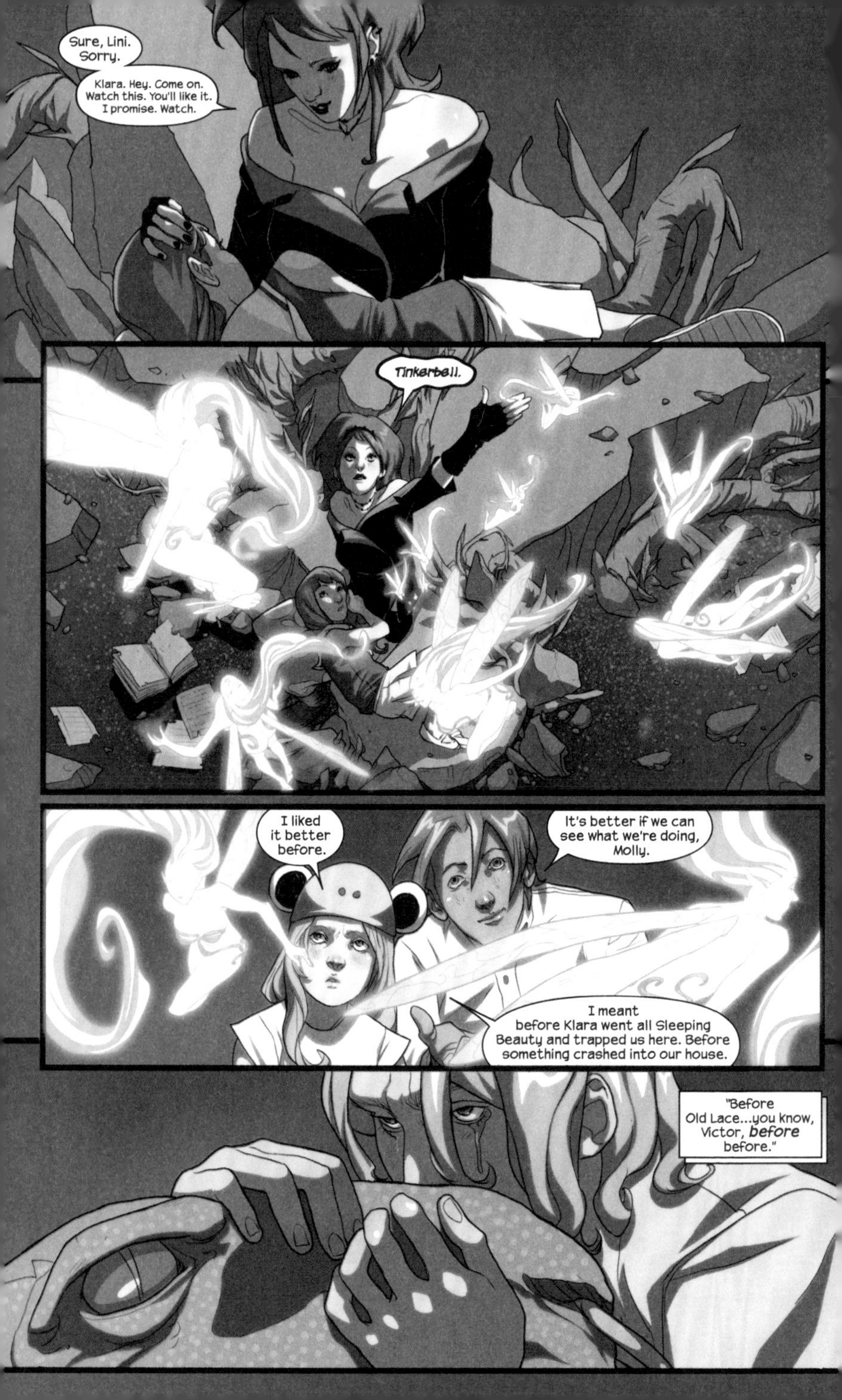

Sure, Lini. Sorry.
Klara. Hey. Come on. Watch this. You'll like it. I promise. Watch.
Tinkerbell.
I liked it better before.
It's better if we can see what we're doing, Molly.
I meant before Klara went all Sleeping Beauty and trapped us here. Before something crashed into our house.
"Before Old Lace...you know, Victor, *before* before."

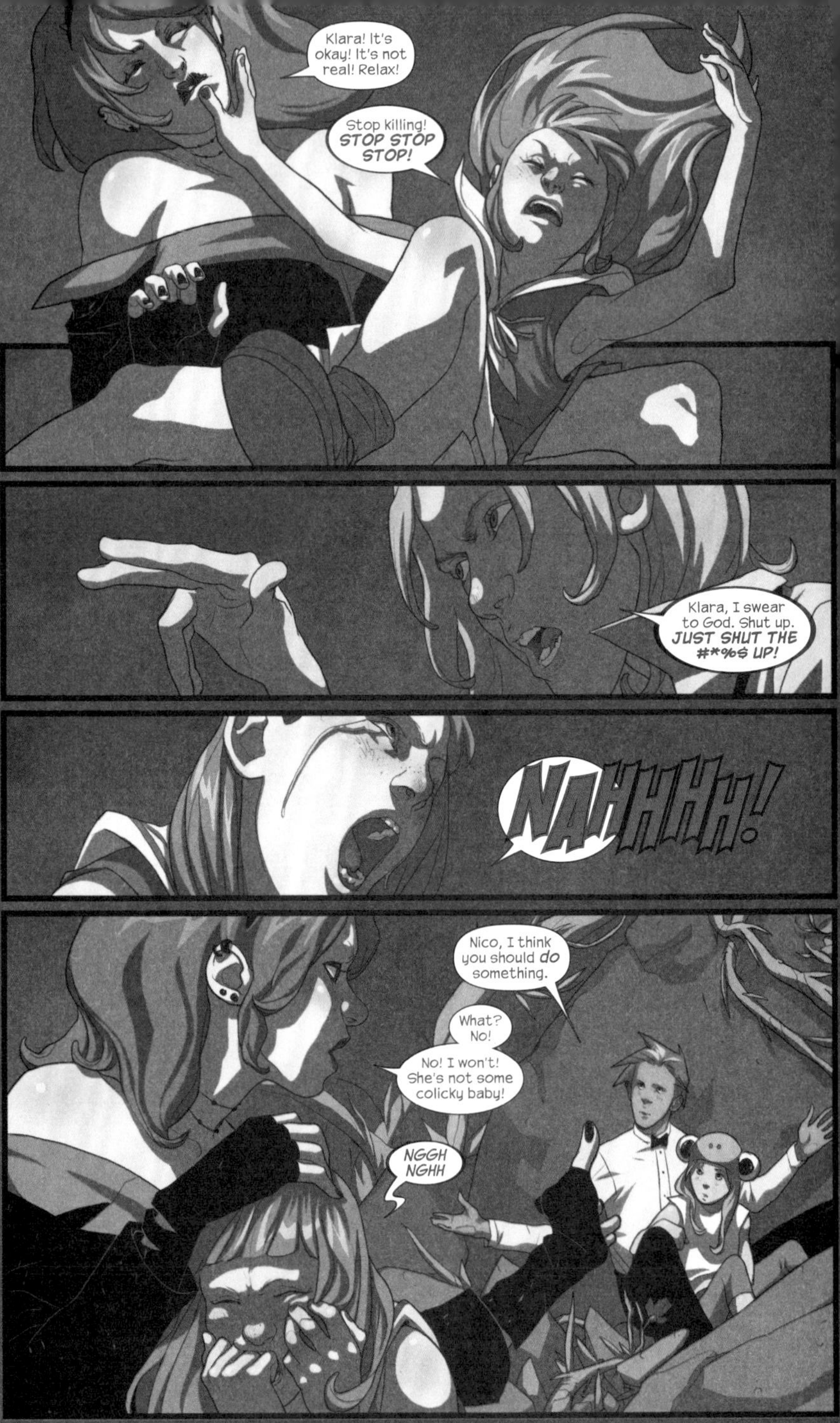
Klara! It's okay! It's not real! Relax!
Stop killing! STOP STOP STOP!
Klara, I swear to God. Shut up. JUST SHUT THE #*%$ UP!
NAHHHH!
Nico, I think you should do something.
What? No!
No! I won't! She's not some colicky baby!
NGGH NGHH

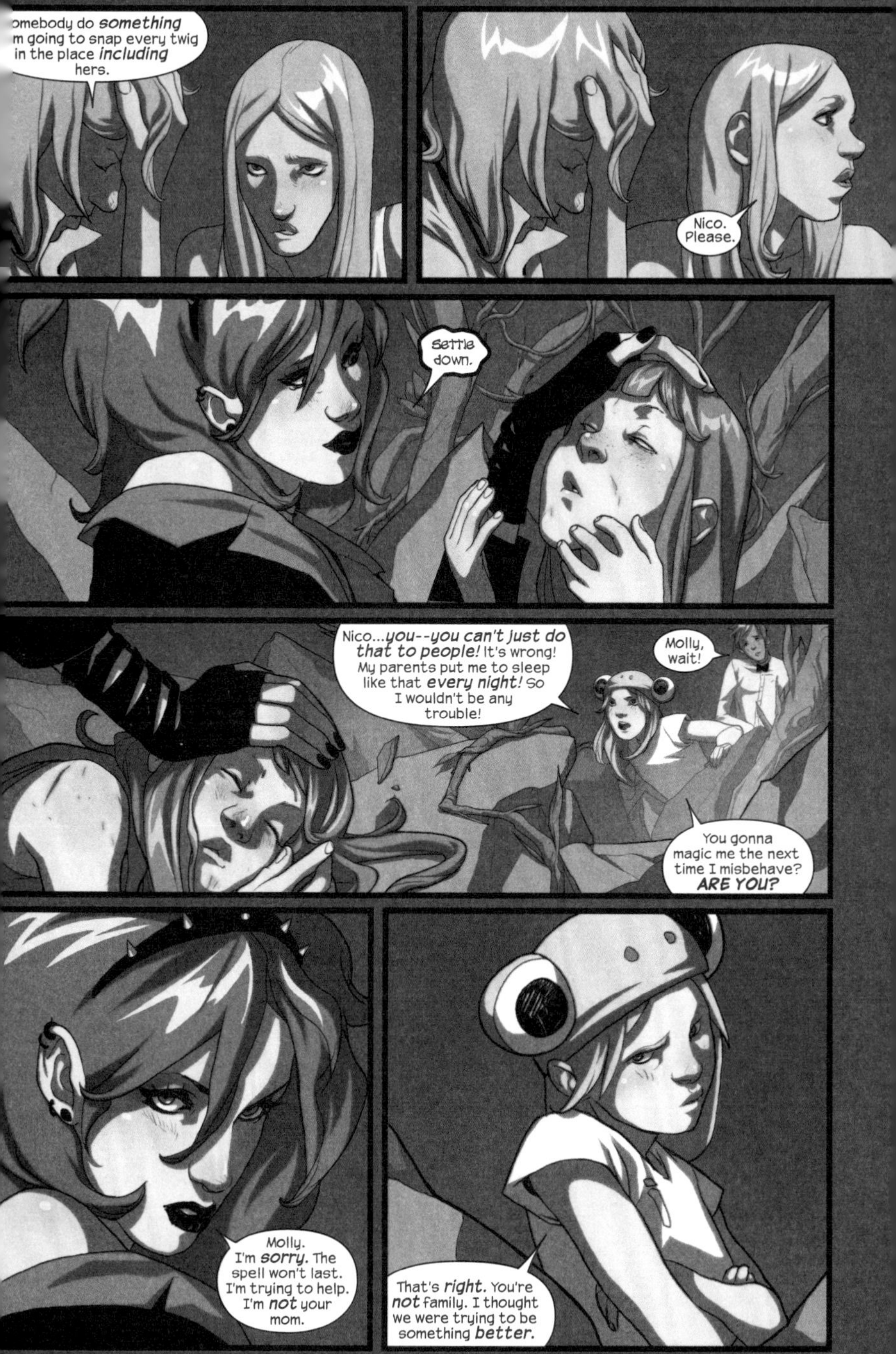

omebody do *something* m going to snap every twig in the place *including* hers.
Nico. Please.
Settle down.
Nico...*you--you can't just do that to people!* It's wrong! My parents put me to sleep like that *every night!* So I wouldn't be any trouble!
Molly, wait!
You gonna magic me the next time I misbehave? **ARE YOU?**
Molly. I'm *sorry*. The spell won't last. I'm trying to help. I'm *not* your mom.
That's *right*. You're *not* family. I thought we were trying to be something *better*.

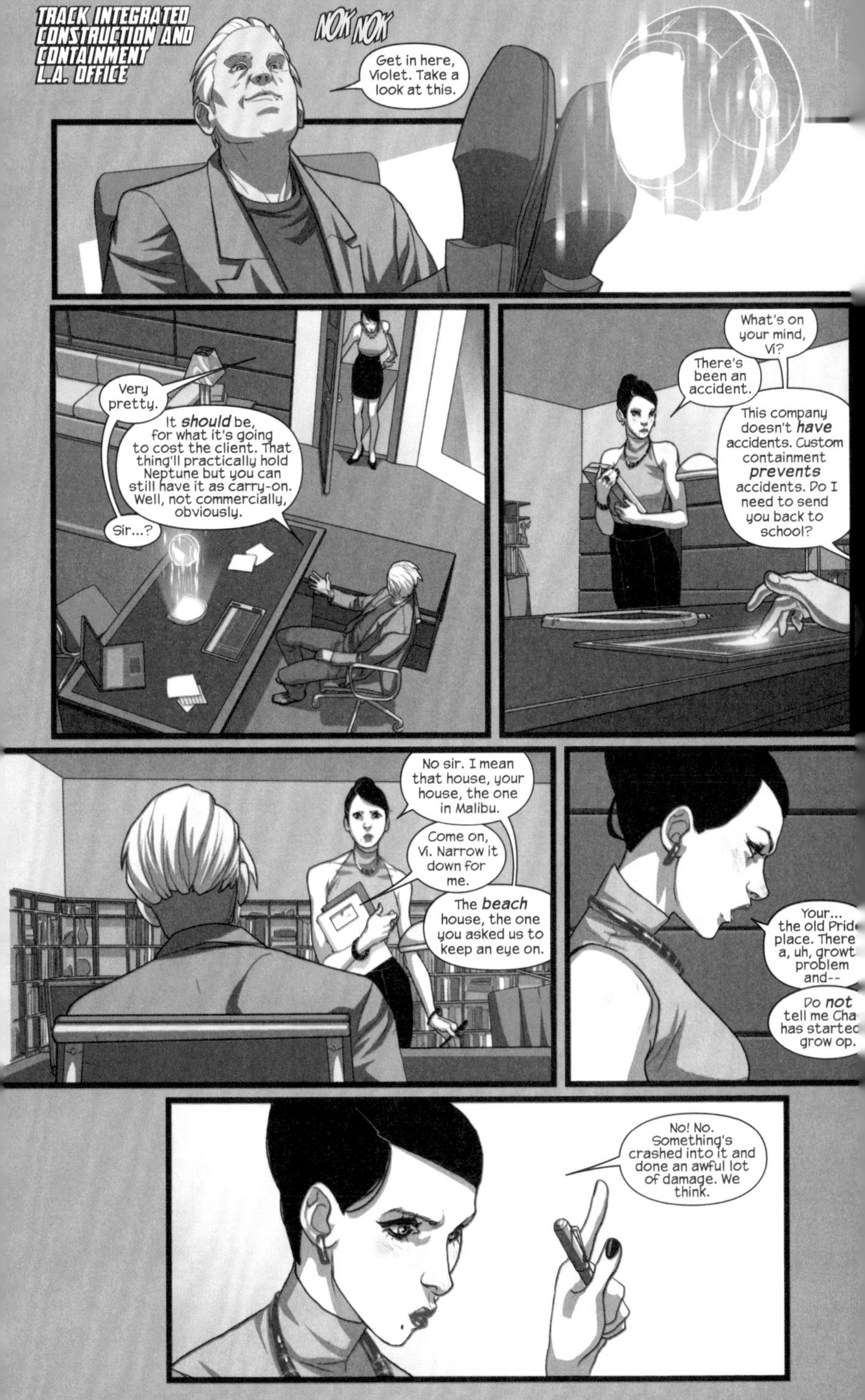
TRACK INTEGRATED CONSTRUCTION AND CONTAINMENT L.A. OFFICE
NOK NOK
Get in here, Violet. Take a look at this.
Very pretty.
It *should* be, for what it's going to cost the client. That thing'll practically hold Neptune but you can still have it as carry-on. Well, not commercially, obviously.
Sir...?
What's on your mind, Vi?
There's been an accident.
This company doesn't *have* accidents. Custom containment *prevents* accidents. Do I need to send you back to school?
No sir. I mean that house, your house, the one in Malibu.
Come on, Vi. Narrow it down for me.
The *beach* house, the one you asked us to keep an eye on.
Your... the old Prid place. There a, uh, growt problem and--
Do *not* tell me Cha has startec grow op.
No! No. Something's crashed into it and done an awful lot of damage. We think.

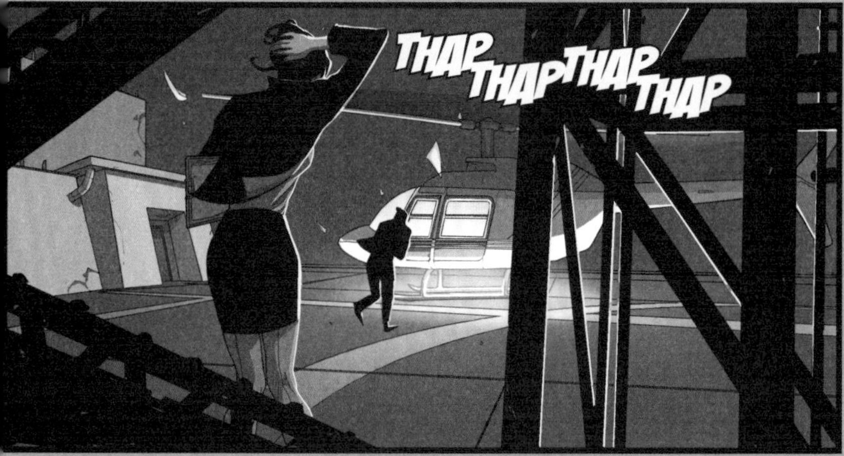
THAP THAP THAP THAP

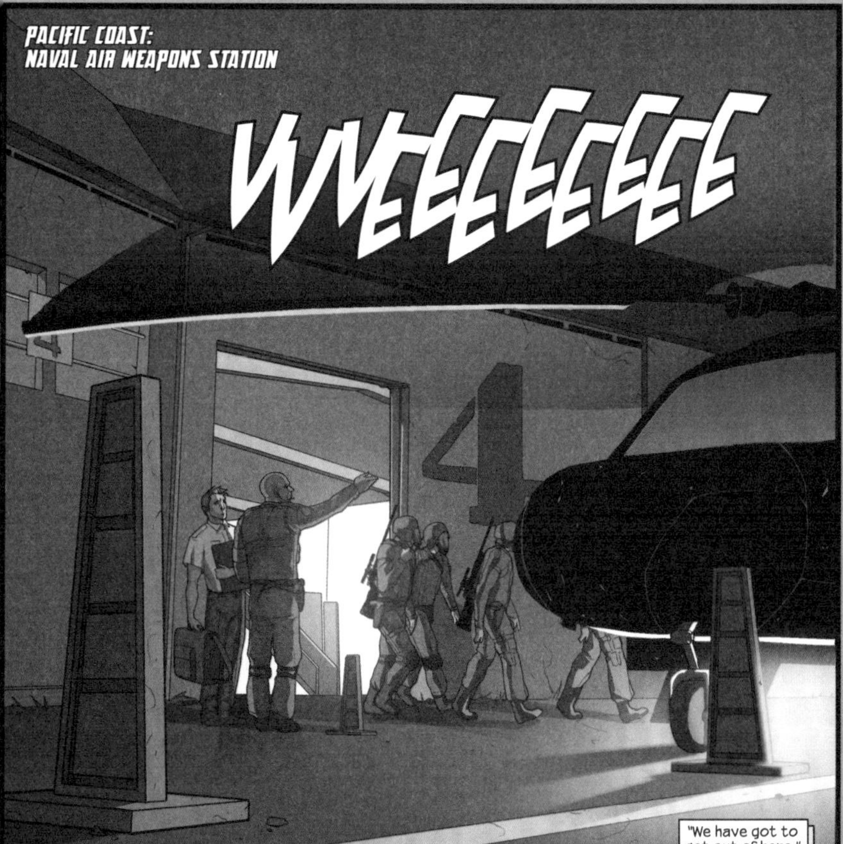
PACIFIC COAST:
NAVAL AIR WEAPONS STATION
WEEEEEEEEE
"We have got to get out of here."

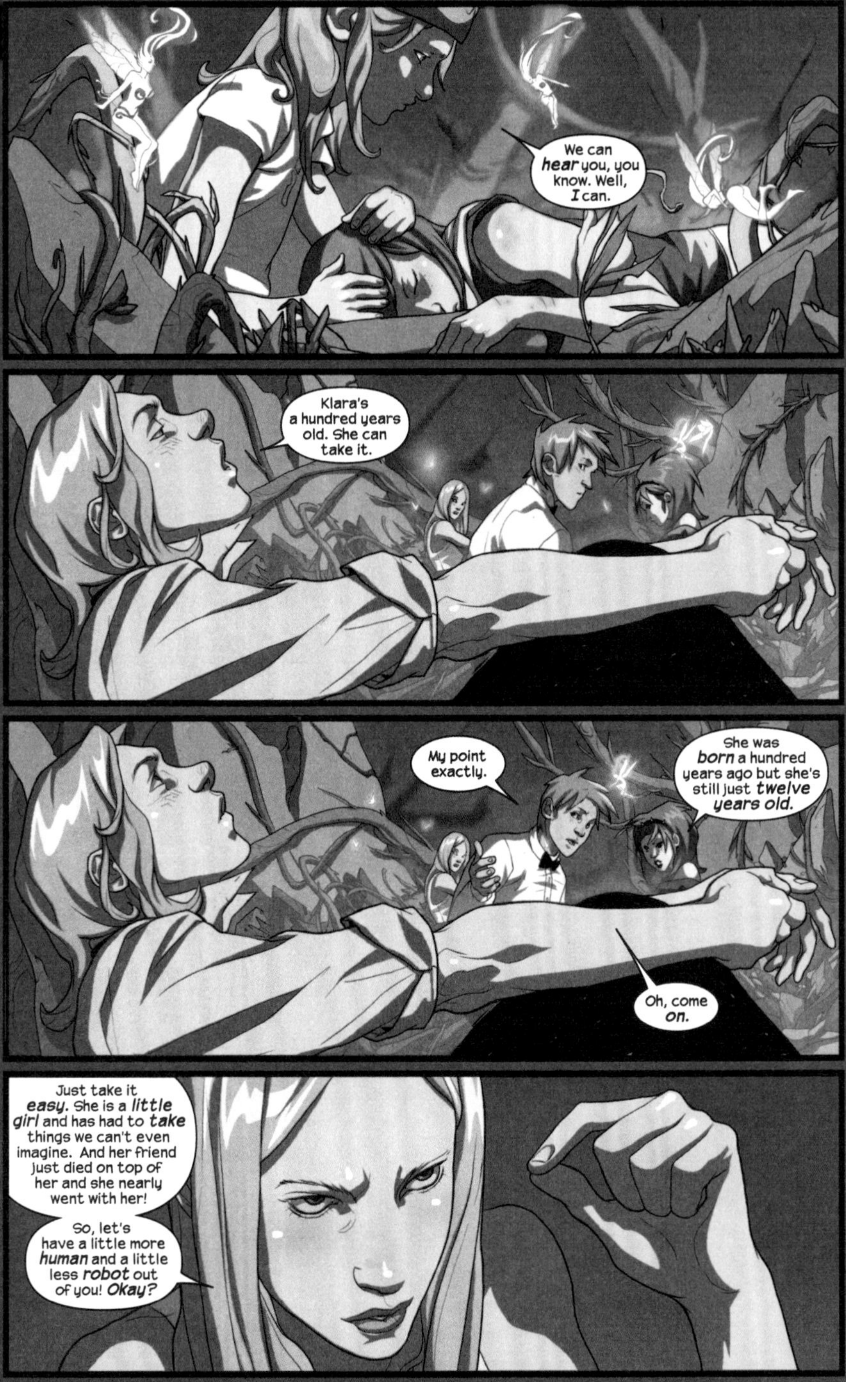

We can hear you, you know. Well, I can.
Klara's a hundred years old. She can take it.
My point exactly.
She was born a hundred years ago but she's still just twelve years old.
Oh, come on.
Just take it easy. She is a little girl and has had to take things we can't even imagine. And her friend just died on top of her and she nearly went with her!
So, let's have a little more human and a little less robot out of you! Okay?

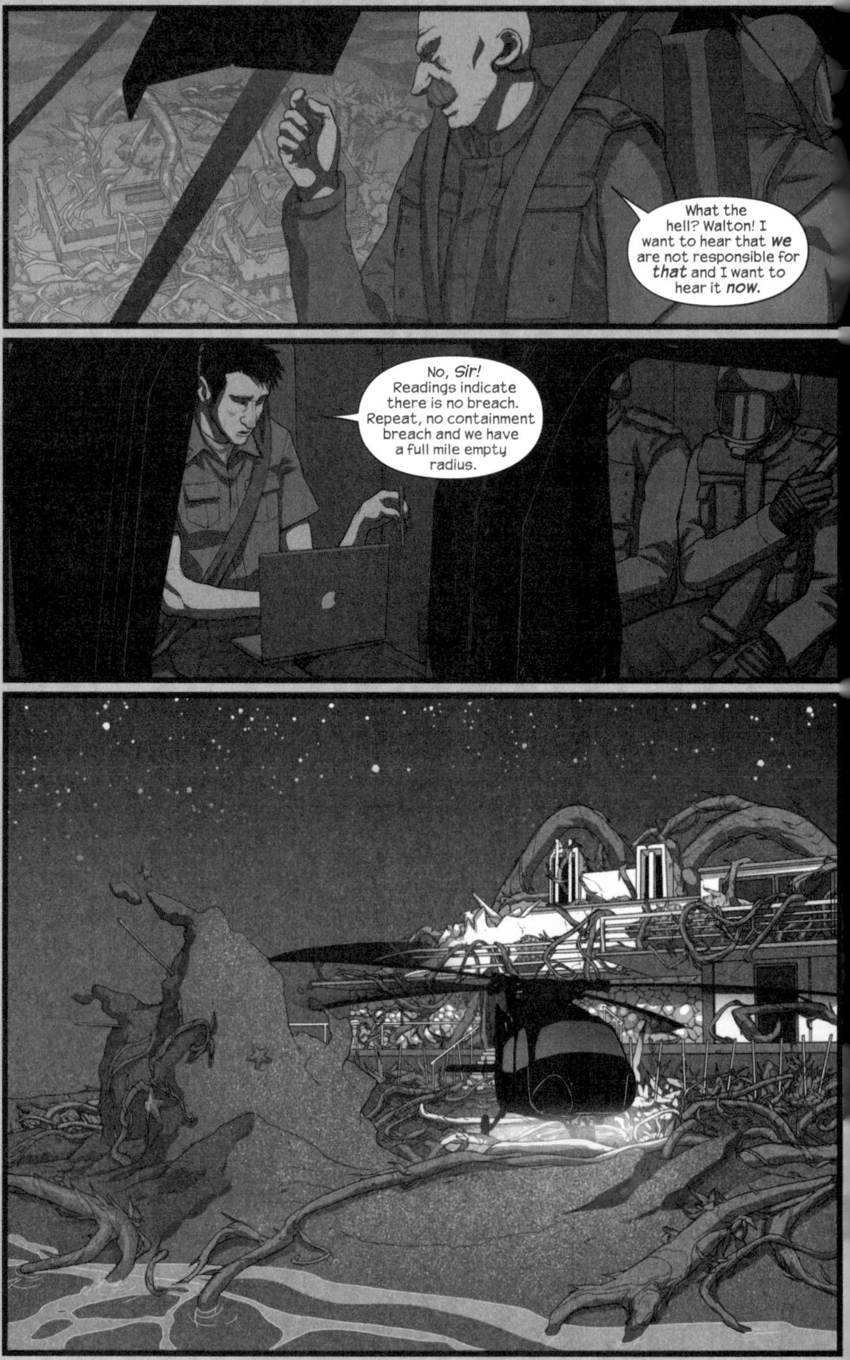
What the hell? Walton! I want to hear that *we* are not responsible for *that* and I want to hear it *now.*
No, *Sir!* Readings indicate there is no breach. Repeat, no containment breach and we have a full mile empty radius.

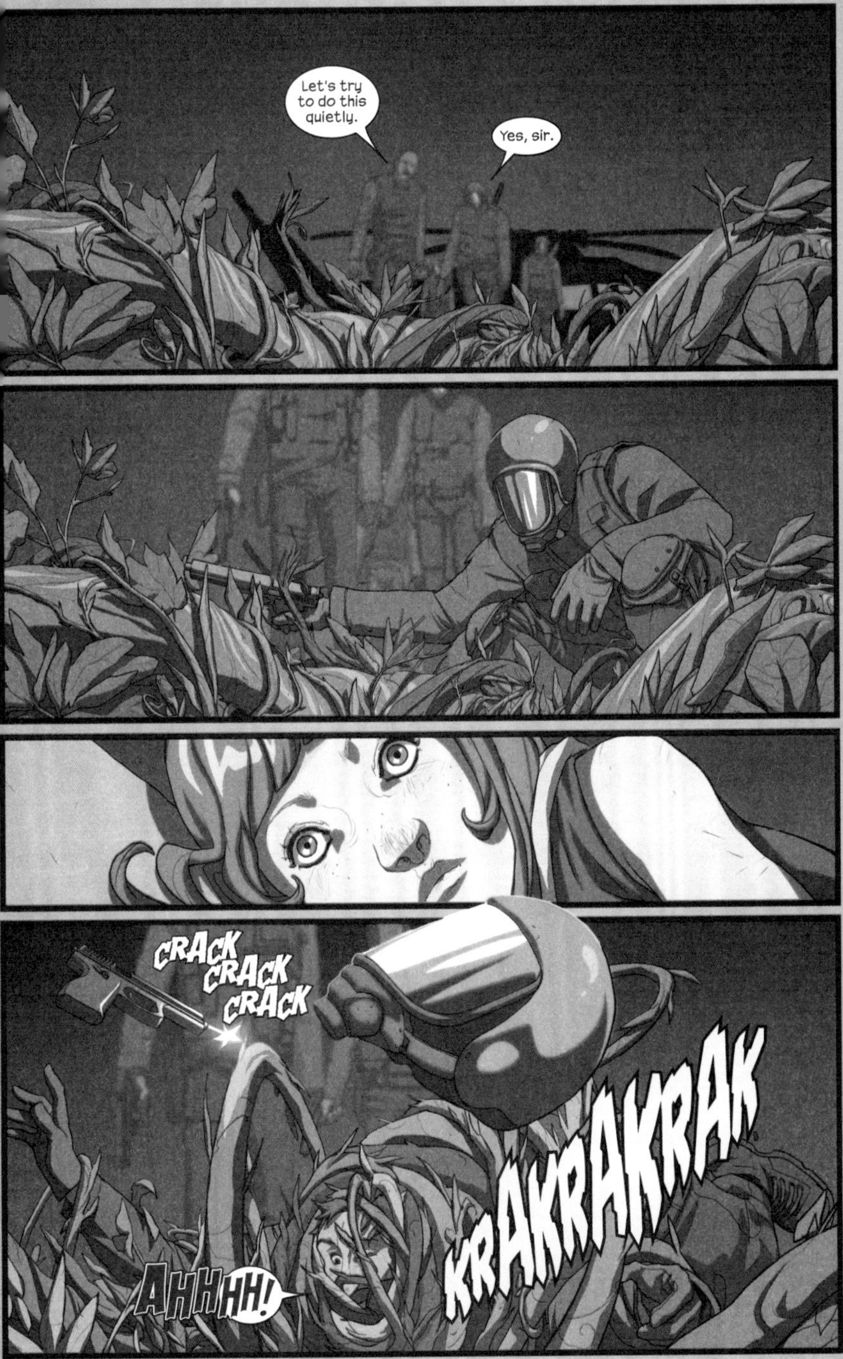

Let's try to do this quietly.
Yes, sir.
CRACK CRACK CRACK
KRAKRAKRAK
AHHHH!

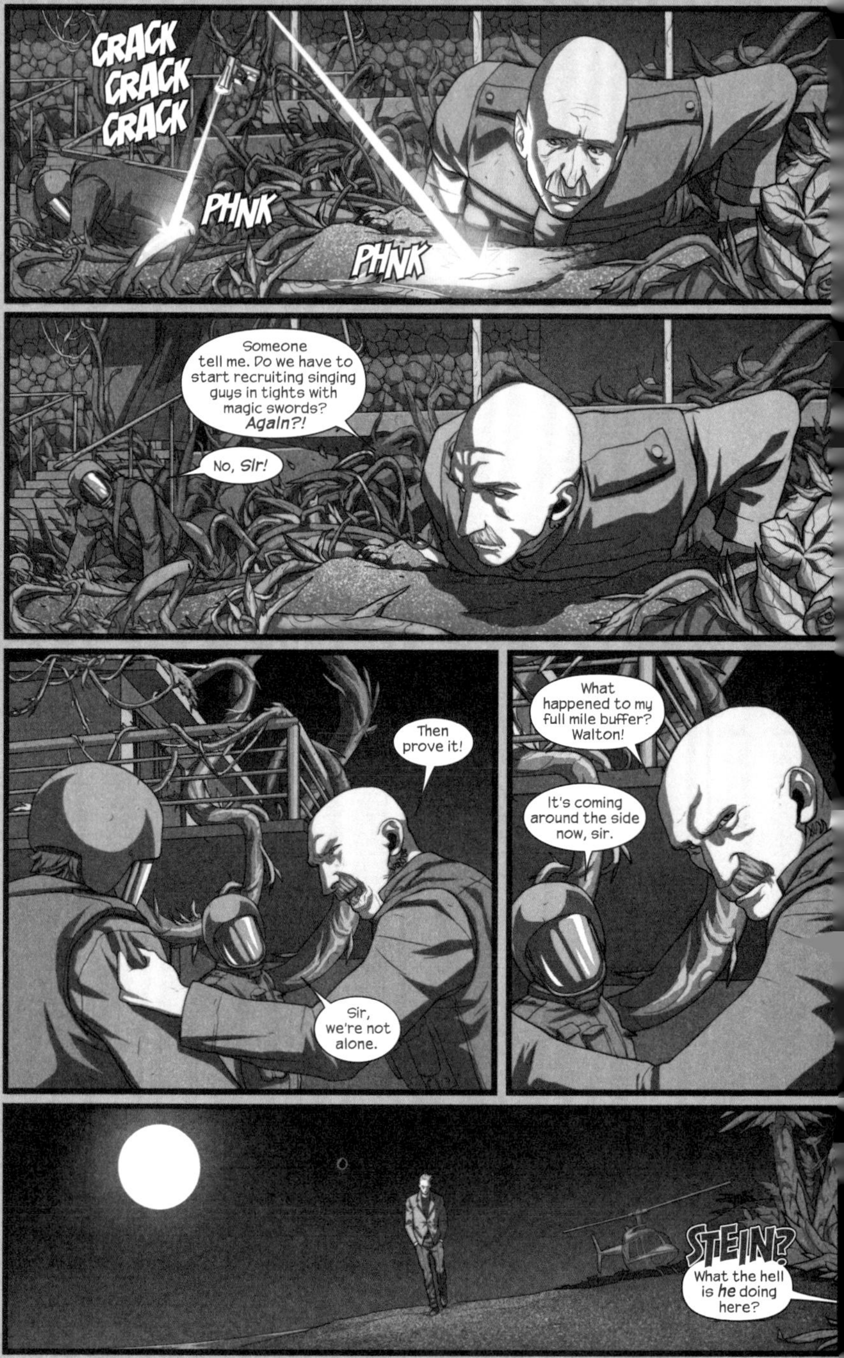
CRACK
CRACK
CRACK
PHNK
PHNK
Someone tell me. Do we have to start recruiting singing guys in tights with magic swords? Again?!
No, Sir!
Then prove it!
Sir, we're not alone.
What happened to my full mile buffer? Walton!
It's coming around the side now, sir.
STEIN?
What the hell is he doing here?

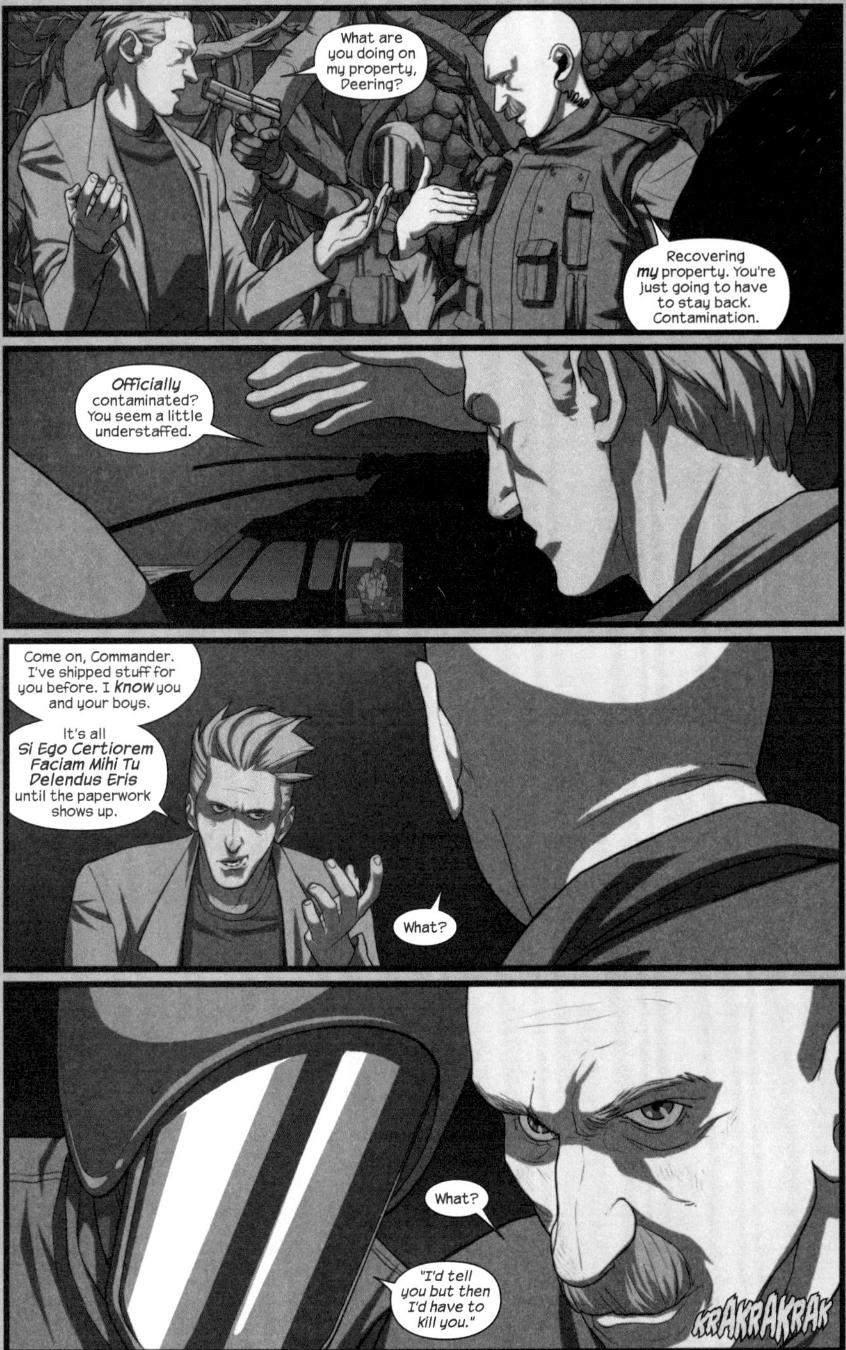

What are you doing on my property, Deering?
Recovering *my* property. You're just going to have to stay back. Contamination.
Officially contaminated? You seem a little understaffed.
Come on, Commander. I've shipped stuff for you before. I *know* you and your boys.
It's all *Si Ego Certiorem Faciam Mihi Tu Delendus Eris* until the paperwork shows up.
What?
What?
"I'd tell you but then I'd have to kill you."
KRAKRAKRAK

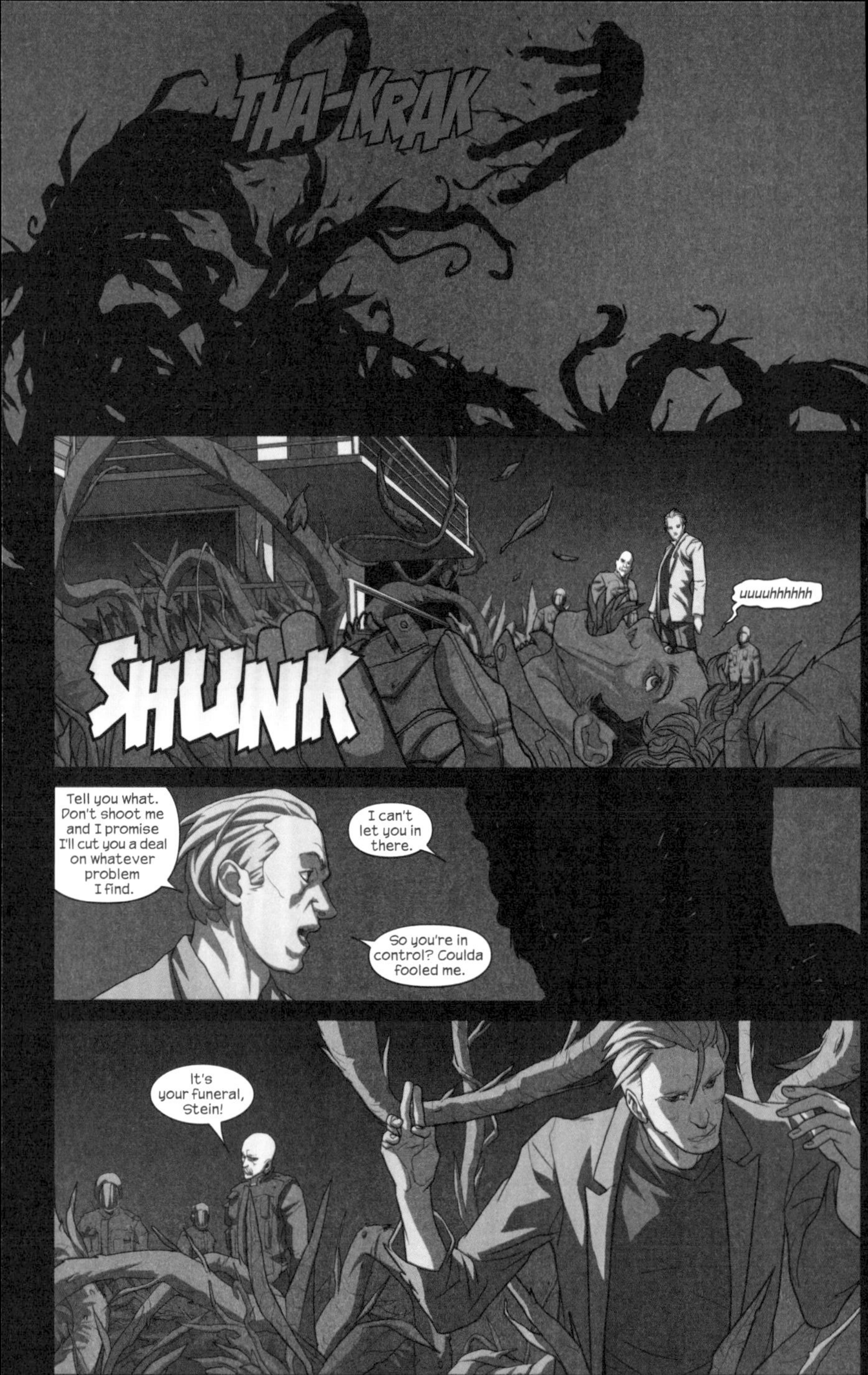
THA-KRAK
SHUNK
uuuuhhhhhh
Tell you what. Don't shoot me and I promise I'll cut you a deal on whatever problem I find.
I can't let you in there.
So you're in control? Coulda fooled me.
It's your funeral, Stein!

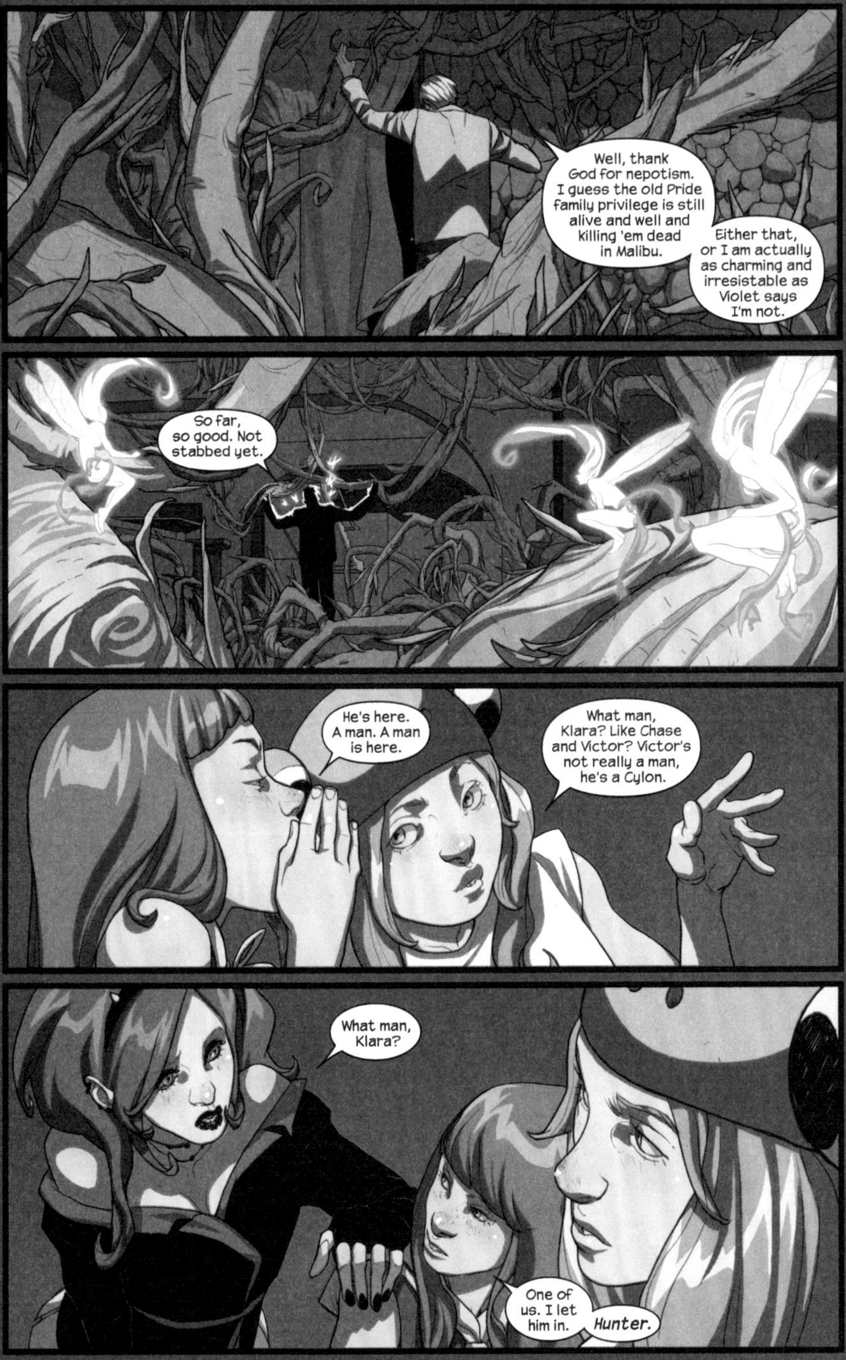
Well, thank God for nepotism. I guess the old Pride family privilege is still alive and well and killing 'em dead in Malibu.
Either that, or I am actually as charming and irresistable as Violet says I'm not.
So far, so good. Not stabbed yet.
He's here. A man. A man is here.
What man, Klara? Like Chase and Victor? Victor's not really a man, he's a Cylon.
What man, Klara?
One of us. I let him in.
Hunter.

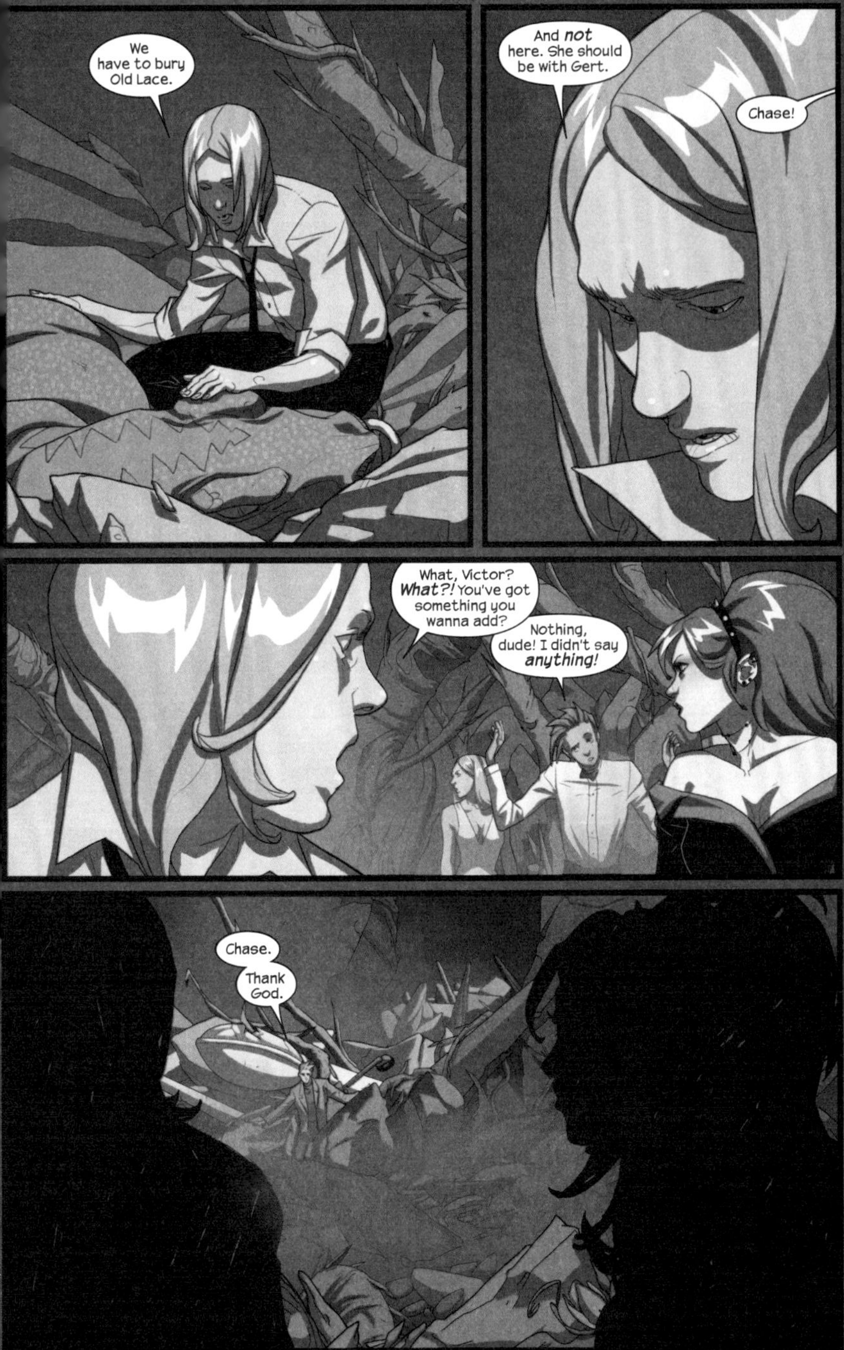
We have to bury Old Lace.
And not here. She should be with Gert.
Chase!
What, Victor? What?! You've got something you wanna add?
Nothing, dude! I didn't say anything!
Chase.
Thank God.

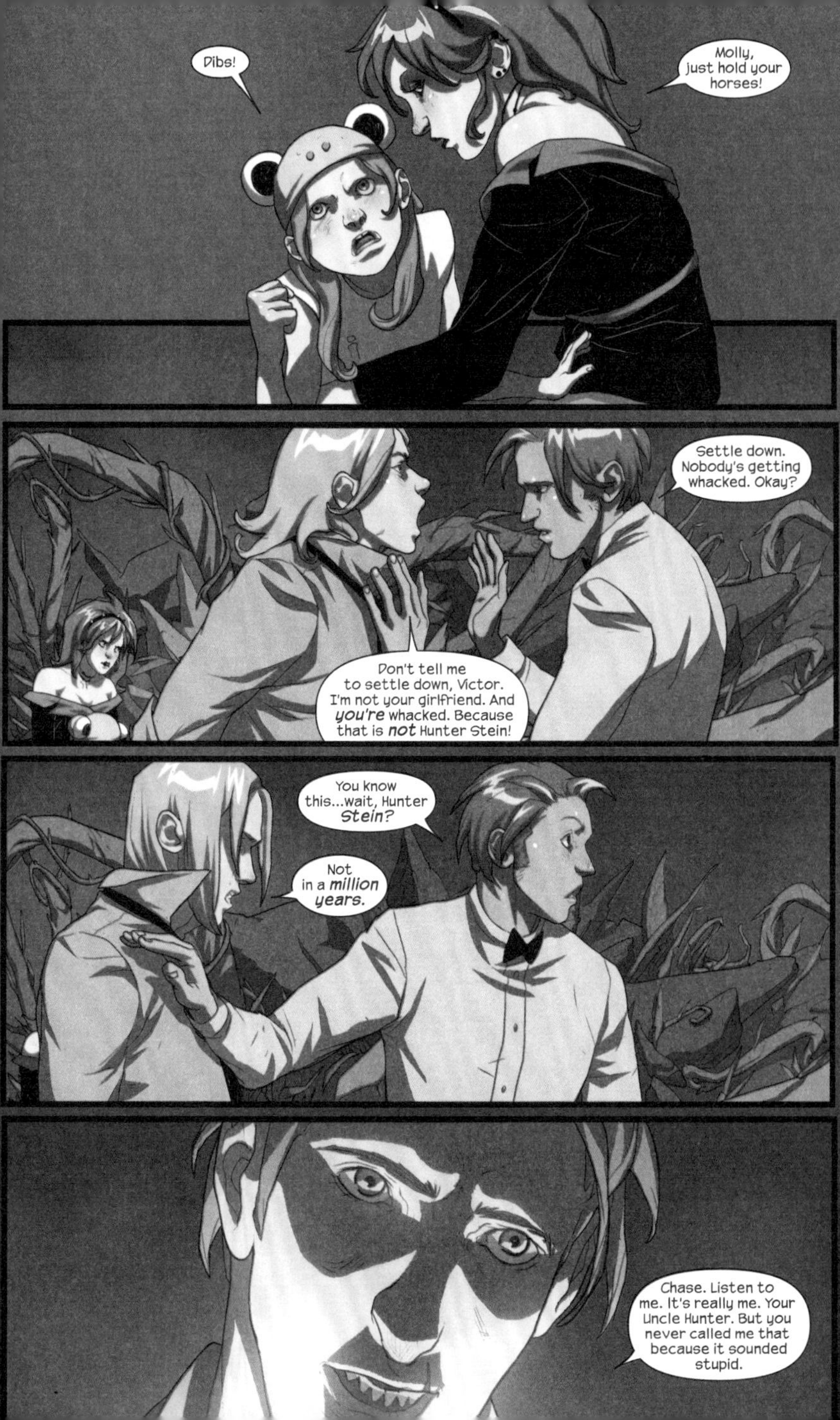
Dibs!
Molly, just hold your horses!
Settle down. Nobody's getting whacked. Okay?
Don't tell me to settle down, Victor. I'm not your girlfriend. And *you're* whacked. Because that is *not* Hunter Stein!
You know this...wait, Hunter *Stein?*
Not in a *million years.*
Chase. Listen to me. It's really me. Your Uncle Hunter. But you never called me that because it sounded stupid.

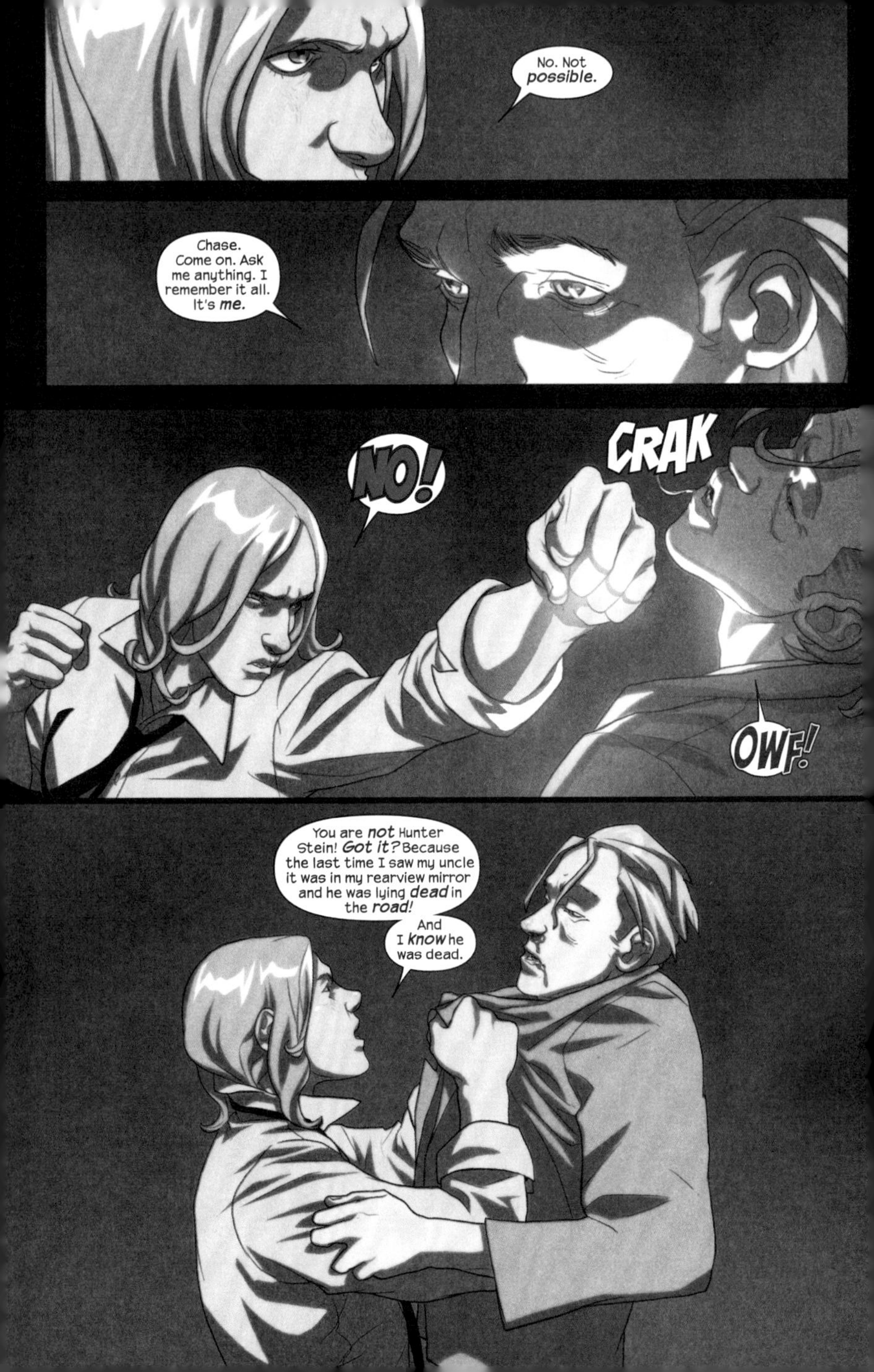
No. Not possible.
Chase. Come on. Ask me anything. I remember it all. It's me.
NO!
CRAK
OWF!
You are not Hunter Stein! Got it? Because the last time I saw my uncle it was in my rearview mirror and he was lying dead in the road!
And I know he was dead.

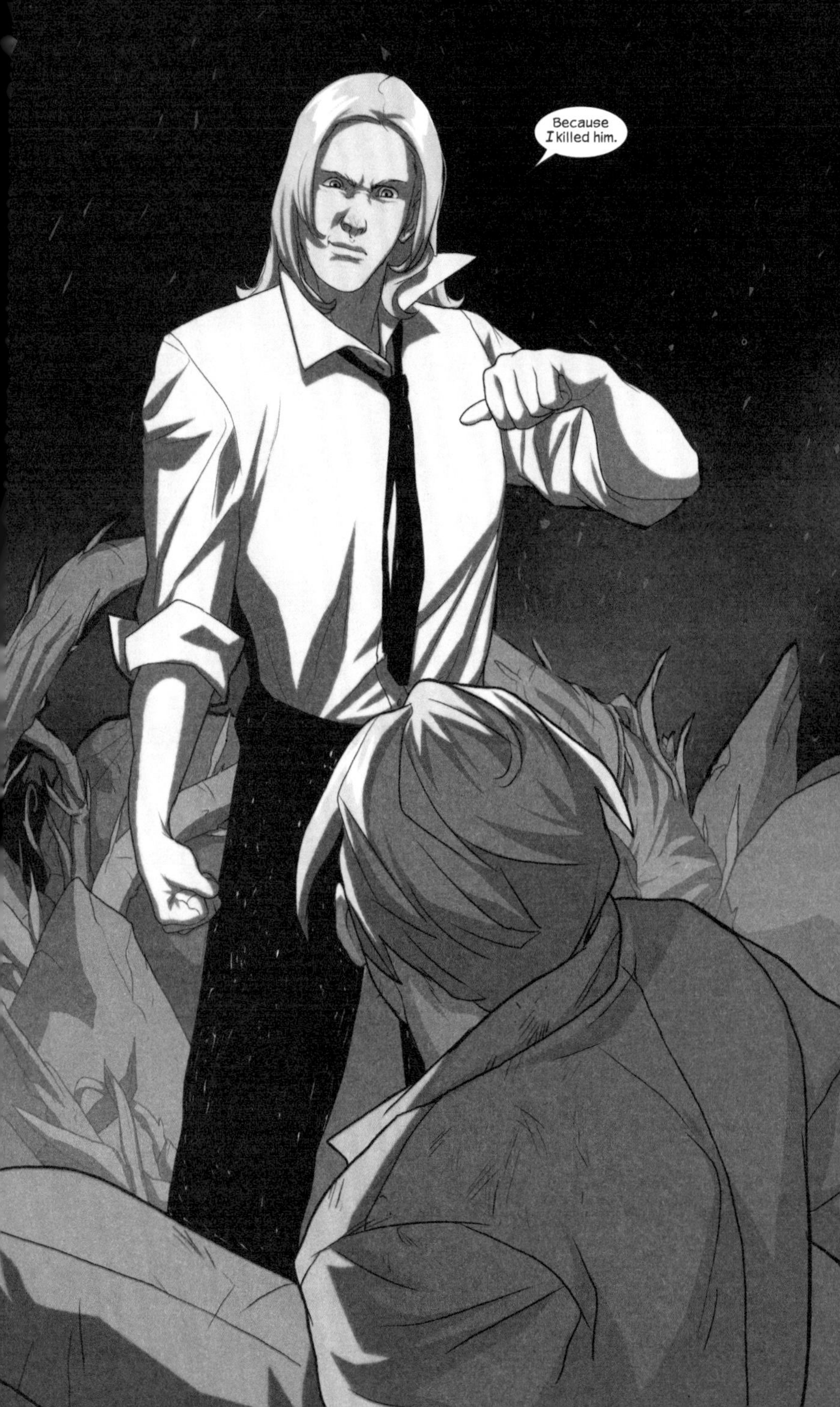
Because *I* killed him.

13

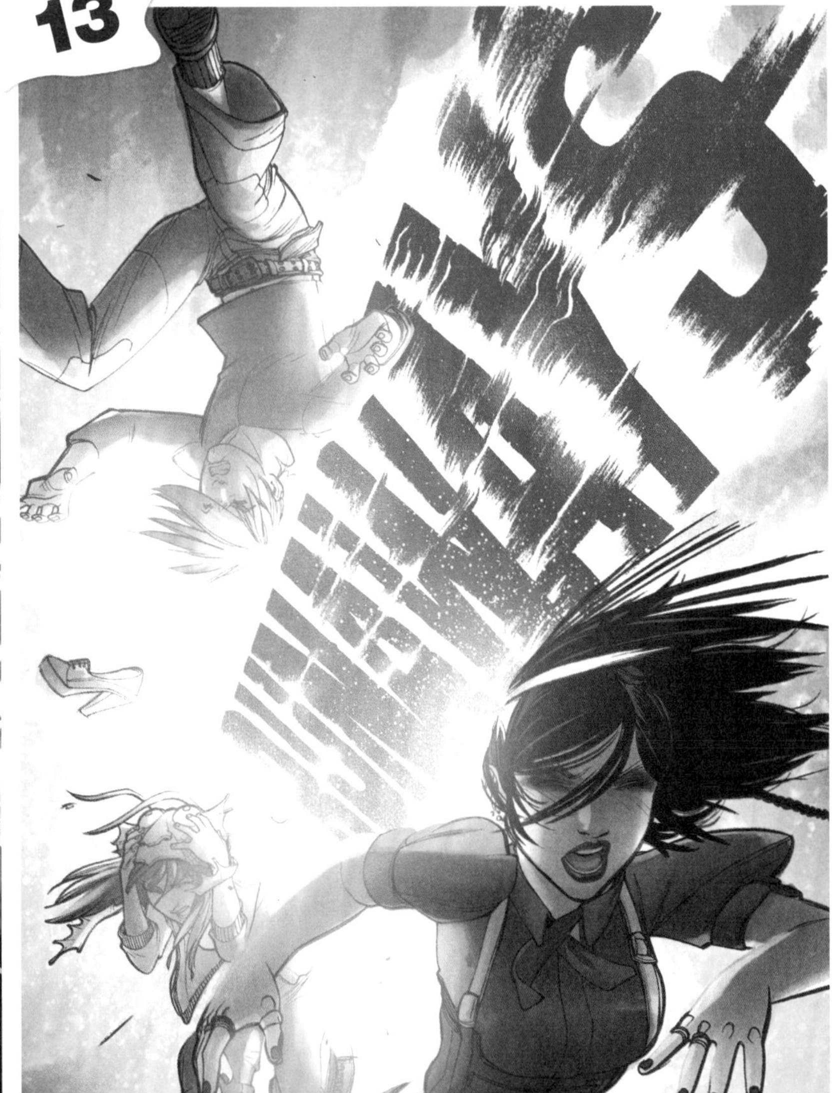

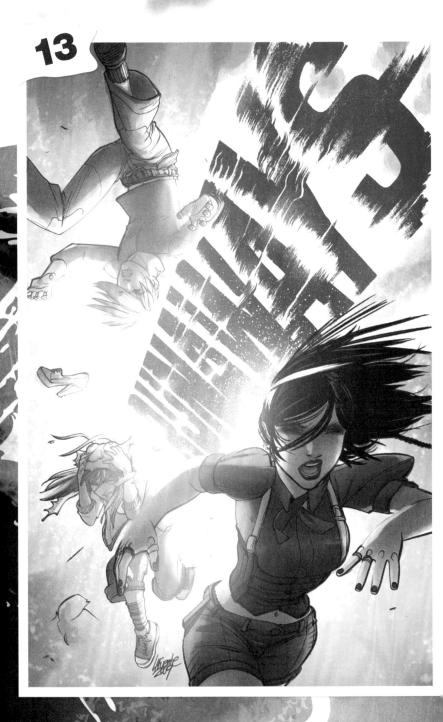

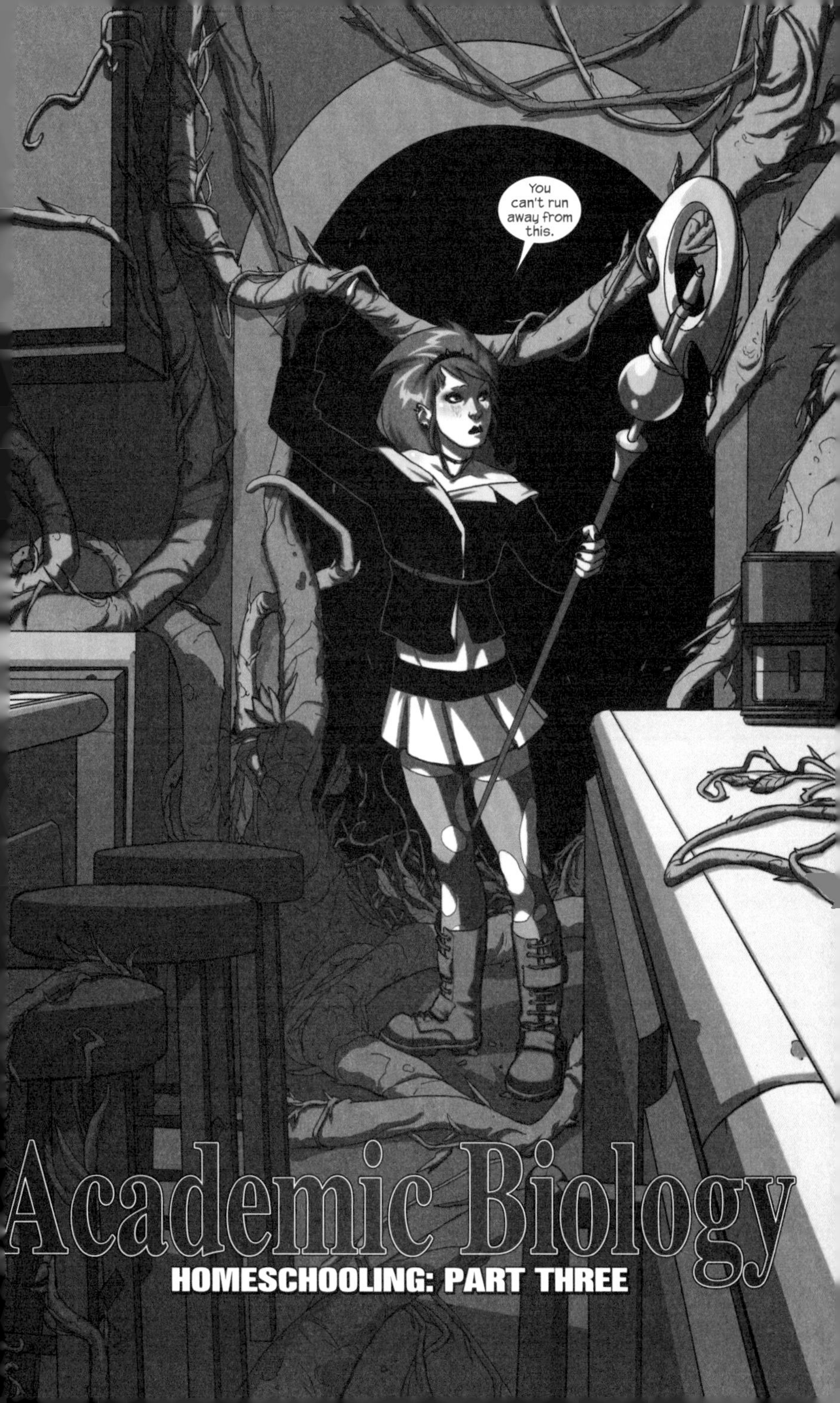
You can't run away from this.
Academic Biology
HOMESCHOOLING: PART THREE

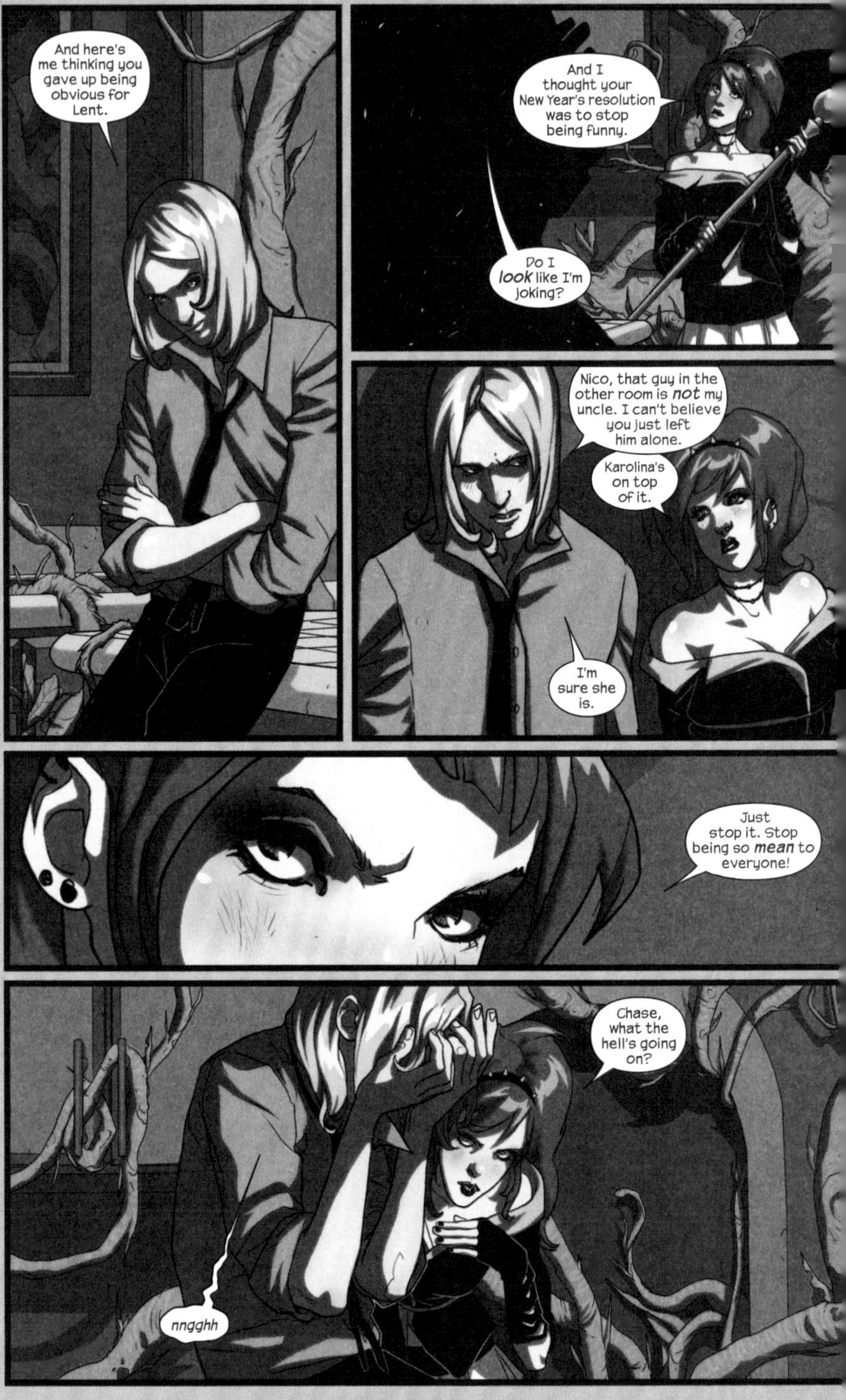
And here's me thinking you gave up being obvious for Lent.
And I thought your New Year's resolution was to stop being funny.
Do I *look* like I'm joking?
Nico, that guy in the other room is *not* my uncle. I can't believe you just left him alone.
Karolina's on top of it.
I'm sure she is.
Just stop it. Stop being so *mean* to everyone!
Chase, what the hell's going on?
nngghh

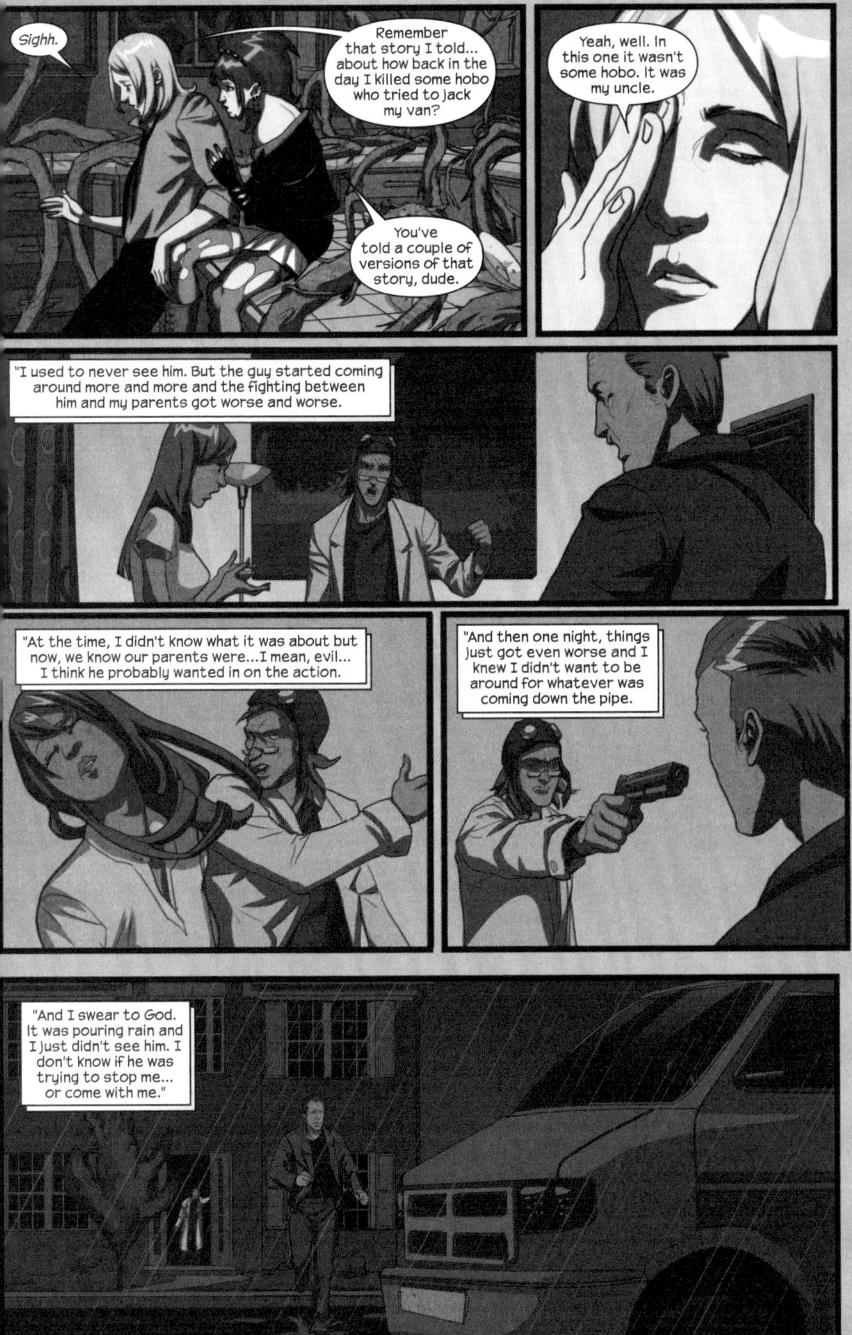
Sighh.
Remember that story I told... about how back in the day I killed some hobo who tried to jack my van?
You've told a couple of versions of that story, dude.
Yeah, well. In this one it wasn't some hobo. It was my uncle.
"I used to never see him. But the guy started coming around more and more and the fighting between him and my parents got worse and worse.
"At the time, I didn't know what it was about but now, we know our parents were...I mean, evil... I think he probably wanted in on the action.
"And then one night, things just got even worse and I knew I didn't want to be around for whatever was coming down the pipe.
"And I swear to God. It was pouring rain and I just didn't see him. I don't know if he was trying to stop me... or come with me."

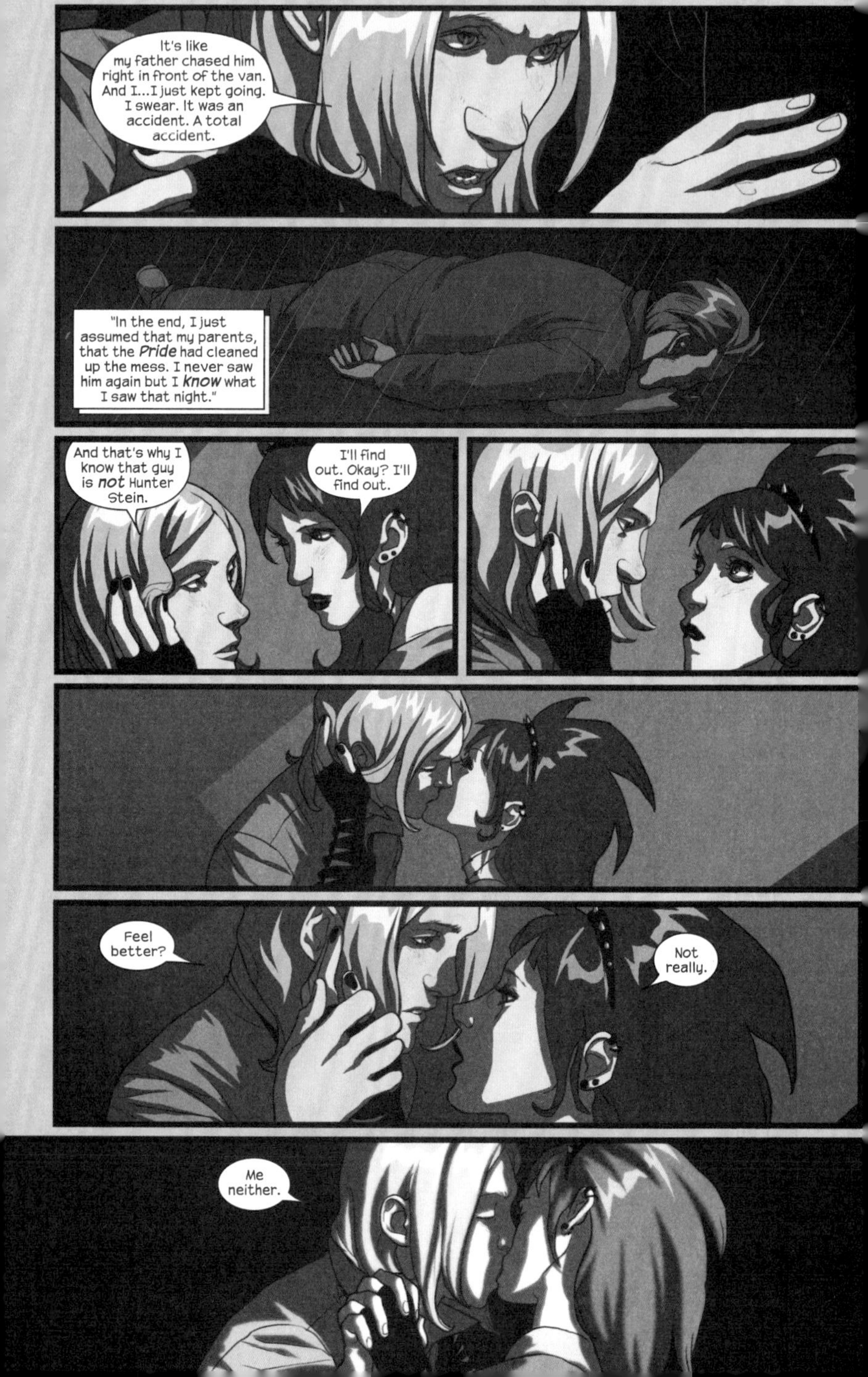

It's like my father chased him right in front of the van. And I...I just kept going. I swear. It was an accident. A total accident.
"In the end, I just assumed that my parents, that the *Pride* had cleaned up the mess. I never saw him again but I *know* what I saw that night."
And that's why I know that guy is *not* Hunter Stein.
I'll find out. Okay? I'll find out.
Feel better?
Not really.
Me neither.

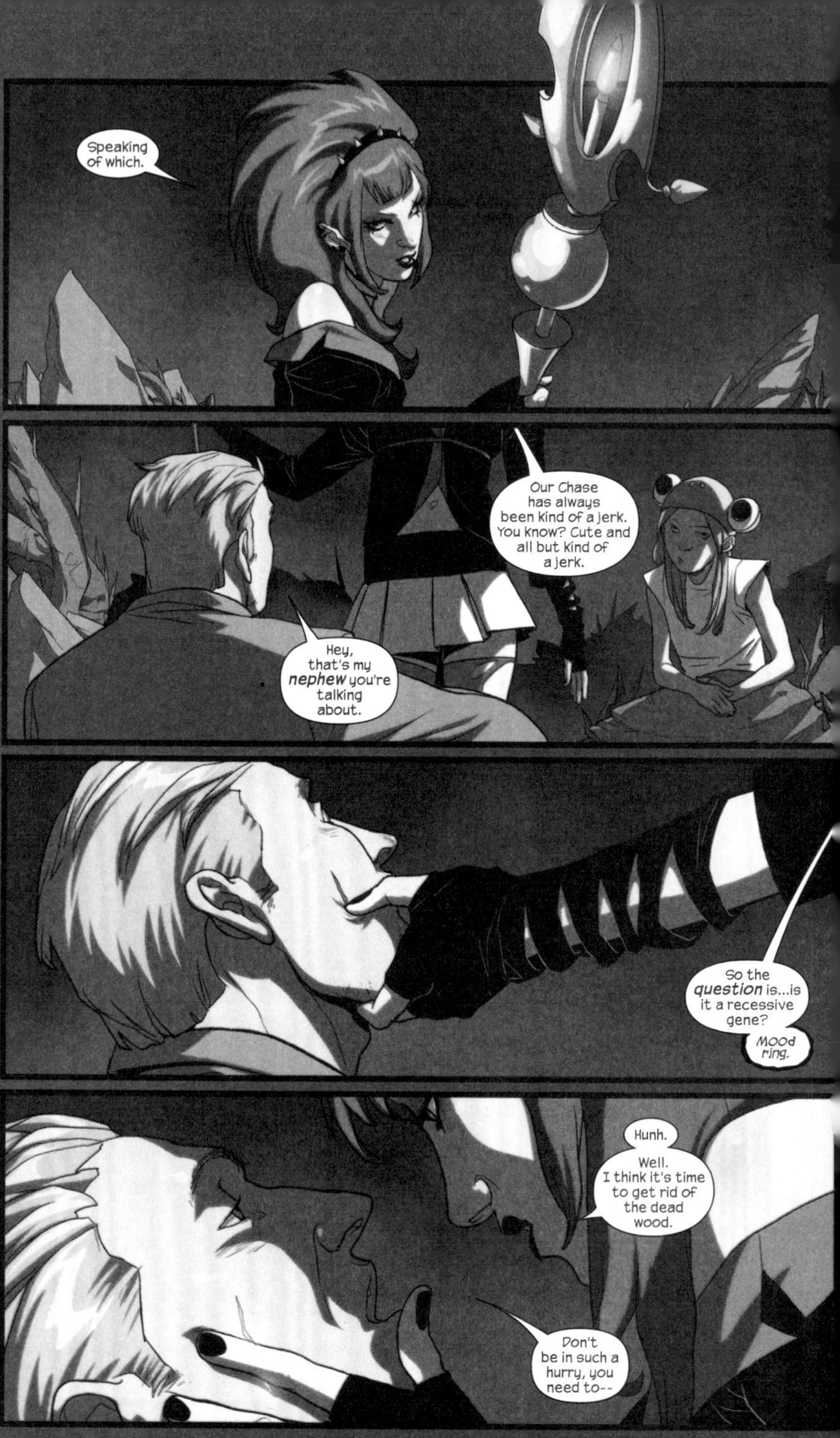
Speaking of which.
Our Chase has always been kind of a jerk. You know? Cute and all but kind of a jerk.
Hey, that's my *nephew* you're talking about.
So the *question* is...is it a recessive gene?
Mood ring.
Hunh.
Well. I think it's time to get rid of the dead wood.
Don't be in such a hurry, you need to--

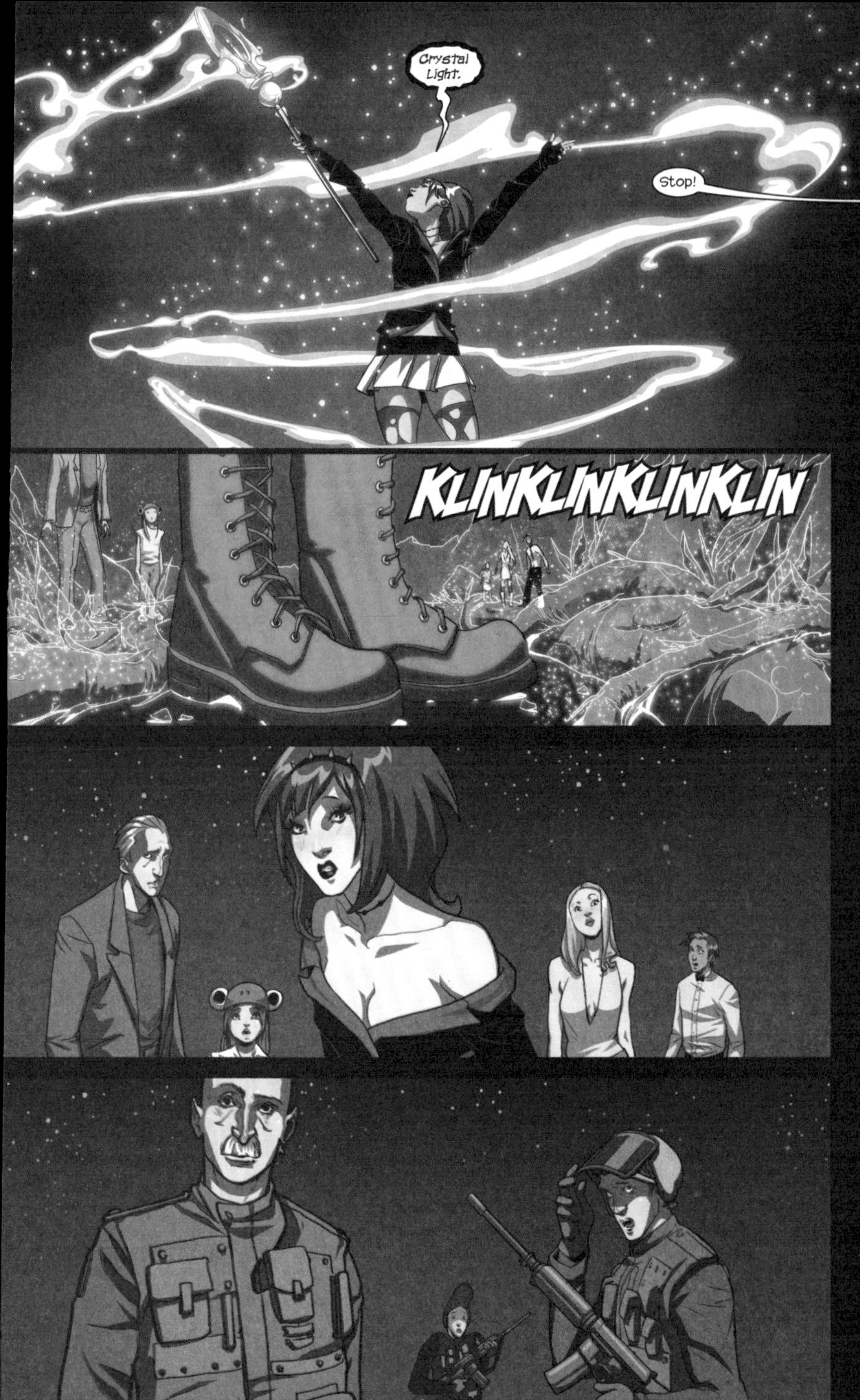
Crystal Light.
Stop!
KLINKLINKLINKLIN

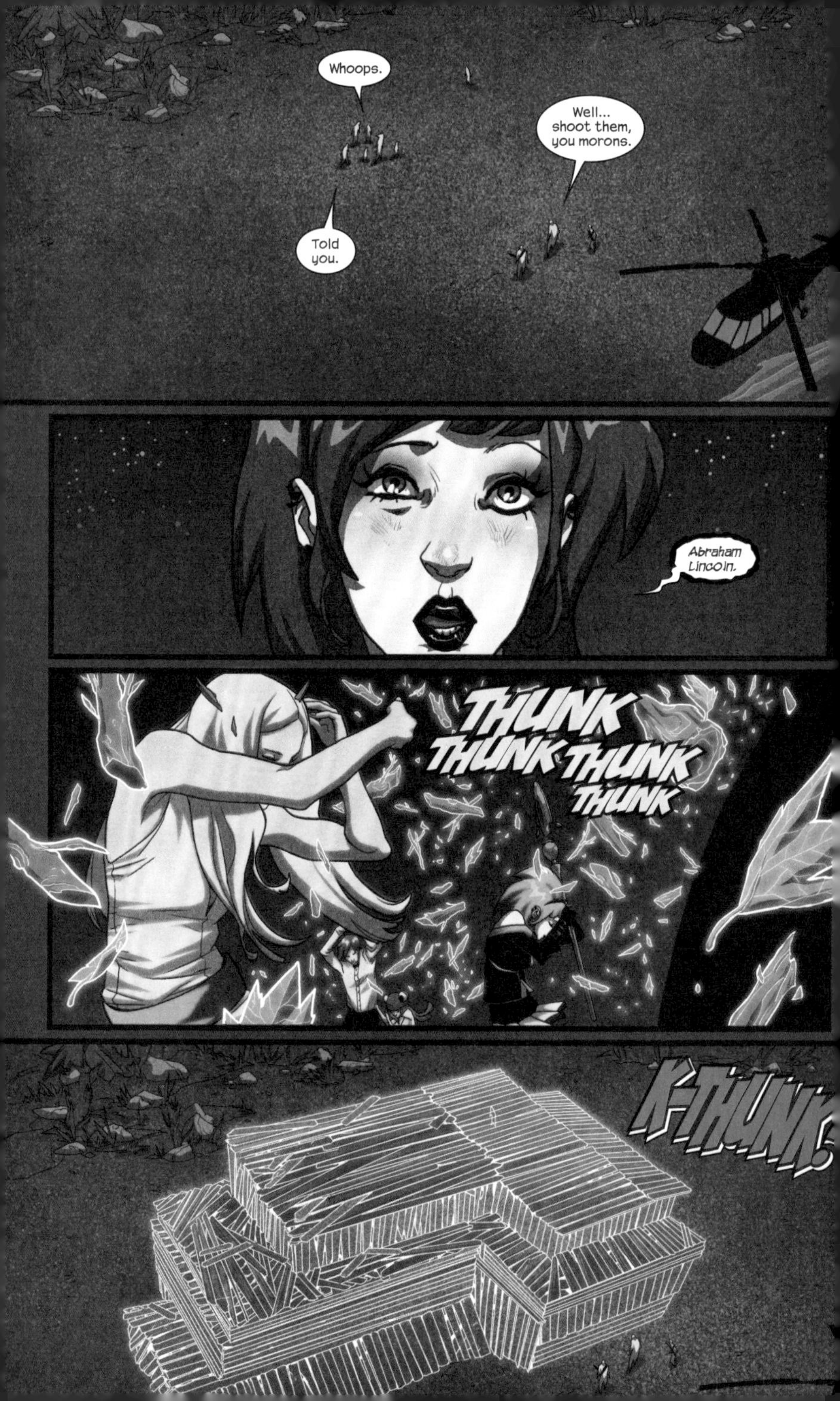
Whoops.
Well... shoot them, you morons.
Told you.
Abraham Lincoln.
THUNK THUNK THUNK THUNK
K-THUNK!

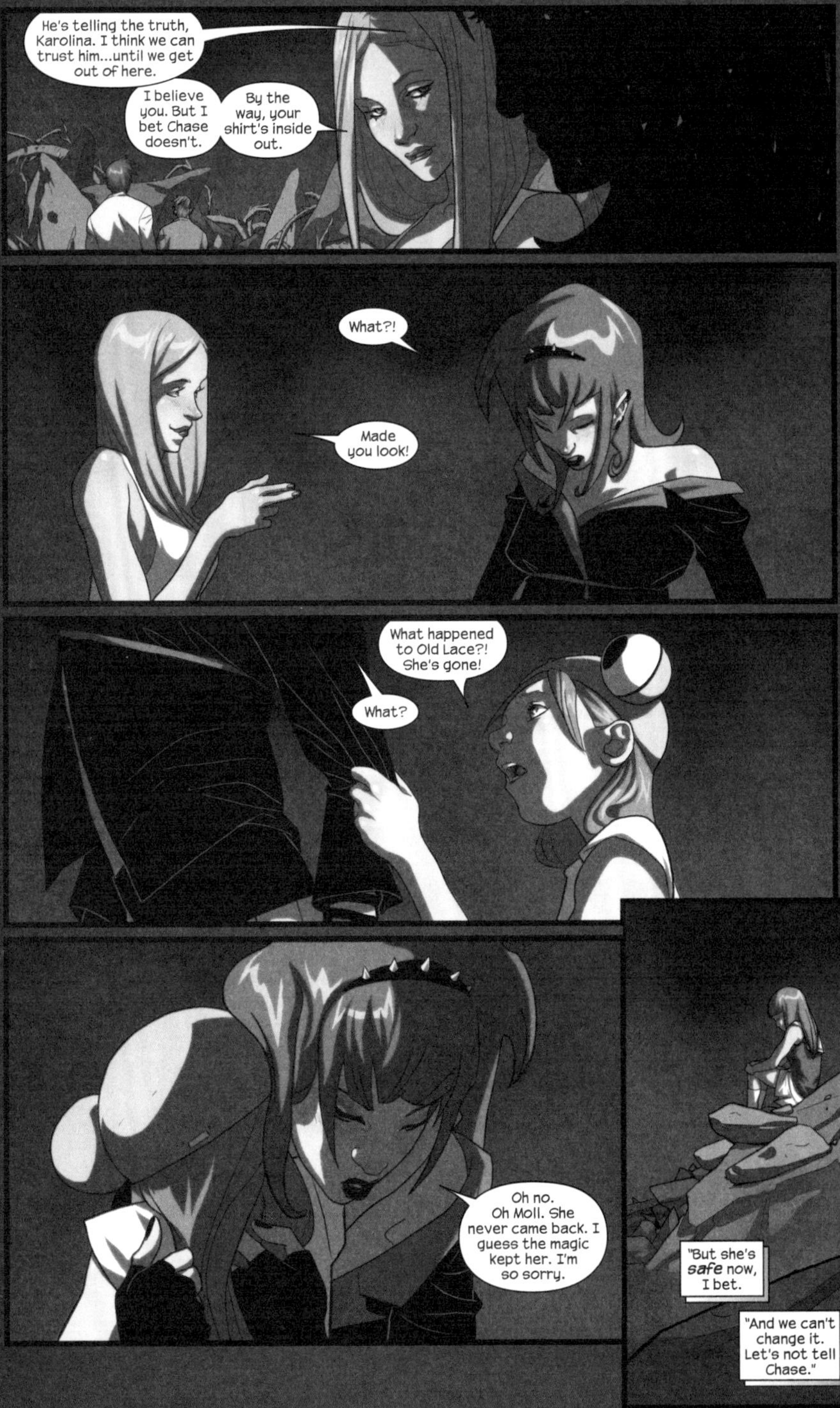
He's telling the truth, Karolina. I think we can trust him...until we get out of here.
I believe you. But I bet Chase doesn't.
By the way, your shirt's inside out.
What?!
Made you look!
What happened to Old Lace?! She's gone!
What?
Oh no. Oh Moll. She never came back. I guess the magic kept her. I'm so sorry.
"But she's *safe* now, I bet.
"And we can't change it. Let's not tell Chase."

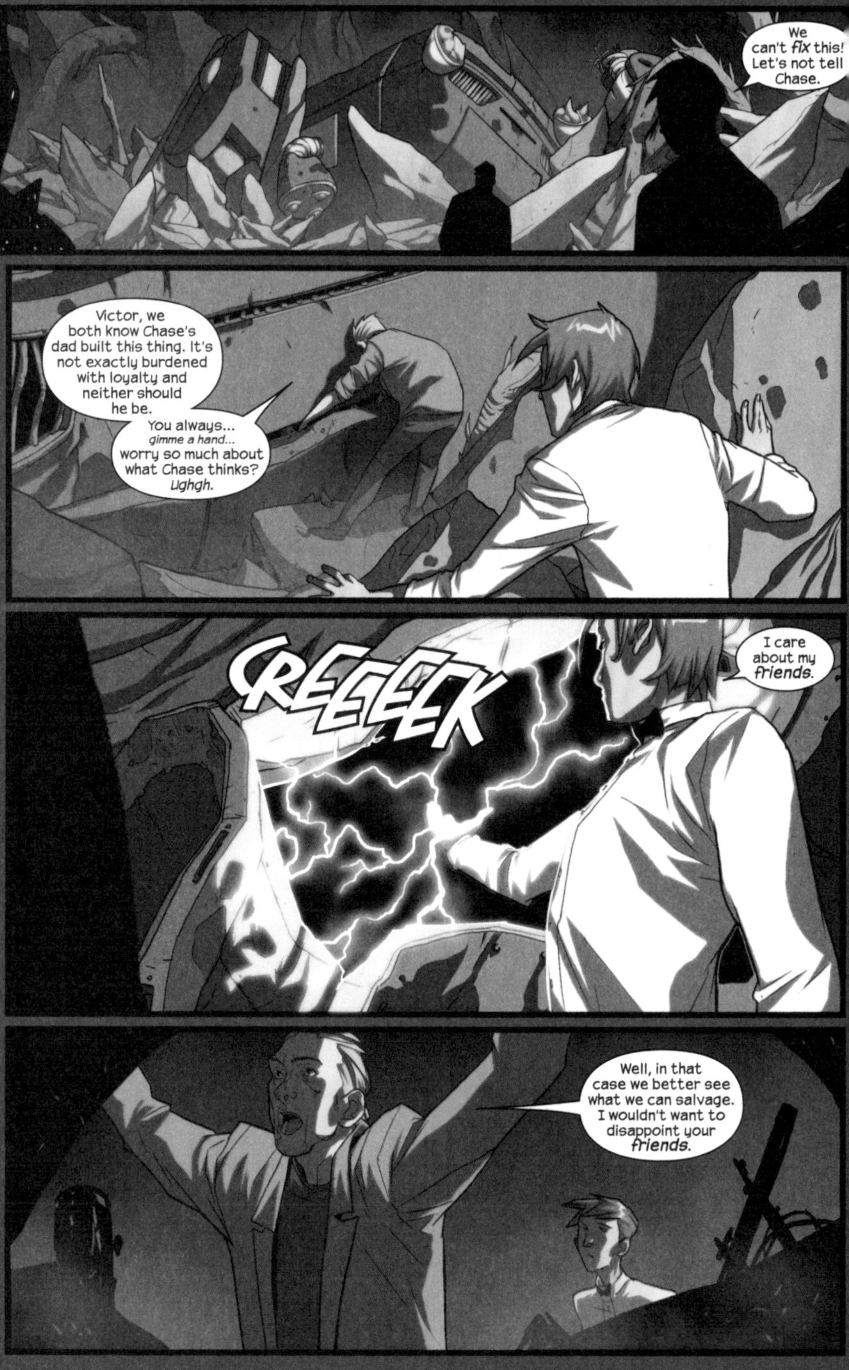
We can't *fix* this! Let's not tell Chase.
Victor, we both know Chase's dad built this thing. It's not exactly burdened with loyalty and neither should he be.
You always... *gimme a hand...* worry so much about what Chase thinks? *Ughgh.*
CREEEEK
I care about my *friends*.
Well, in that case we better see what we can salvage. I wouldn't want to disappoint your *friends*.

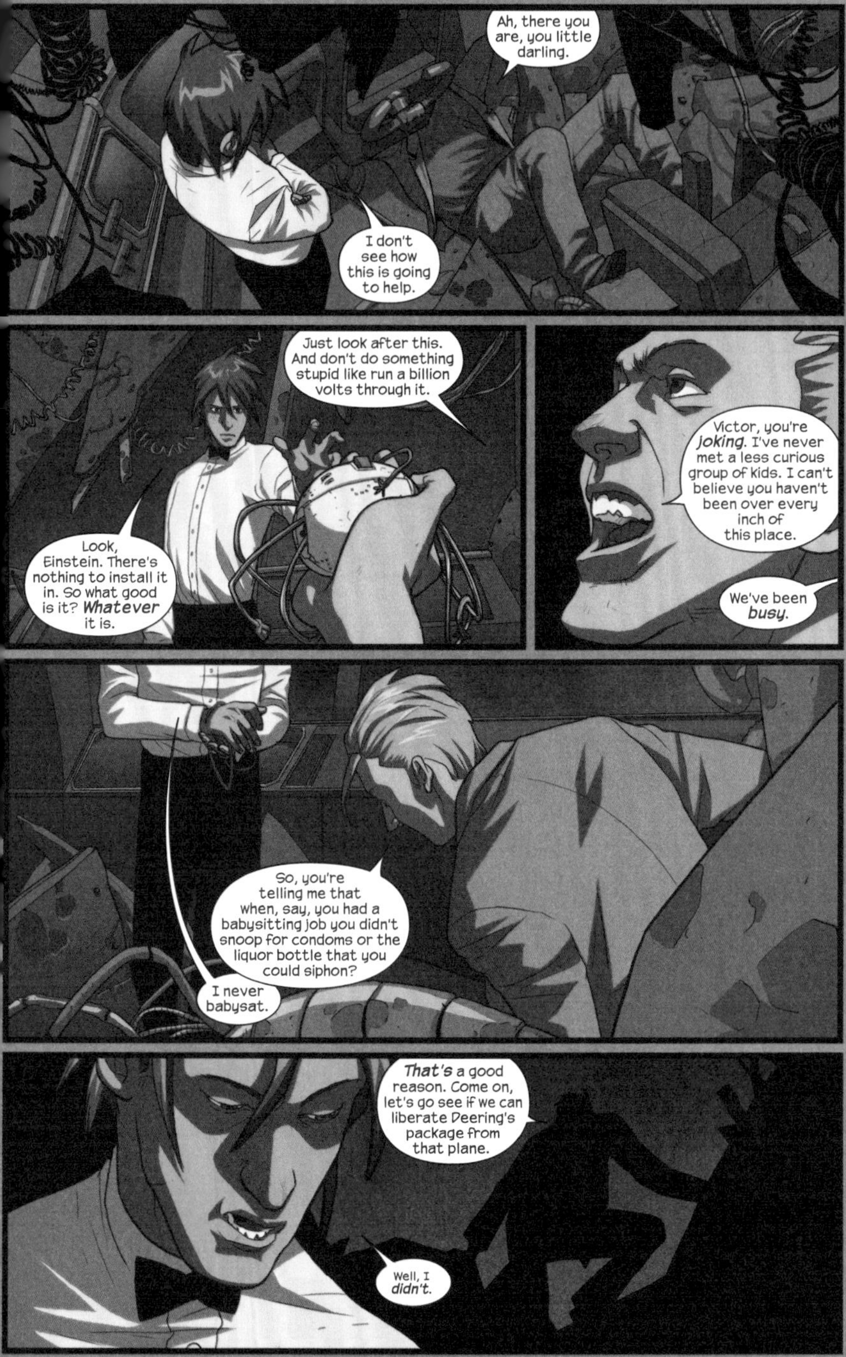
Ah, there you are, you little darling.
I don't see how this is going to help.
Just look after this. And don't do something stupid like run a billion volts through it.
Look, Einstein. There's nothing to install it in. So what good is it? *Whatever* it is.
Victor, you're *joking*. I've never met a less curious group of kids. I can't believe you haven't been over every inch of this place.
We've been *busy*.
So, you're telling me that when, say, you had a babysitting job you didn't snoop for condoms or the liquor bottle that you could siphon?
I never babysat.
That's a good reason. Come on, let's go see if we can liberate Deering's package from that plane.
Well, I *didn't*.

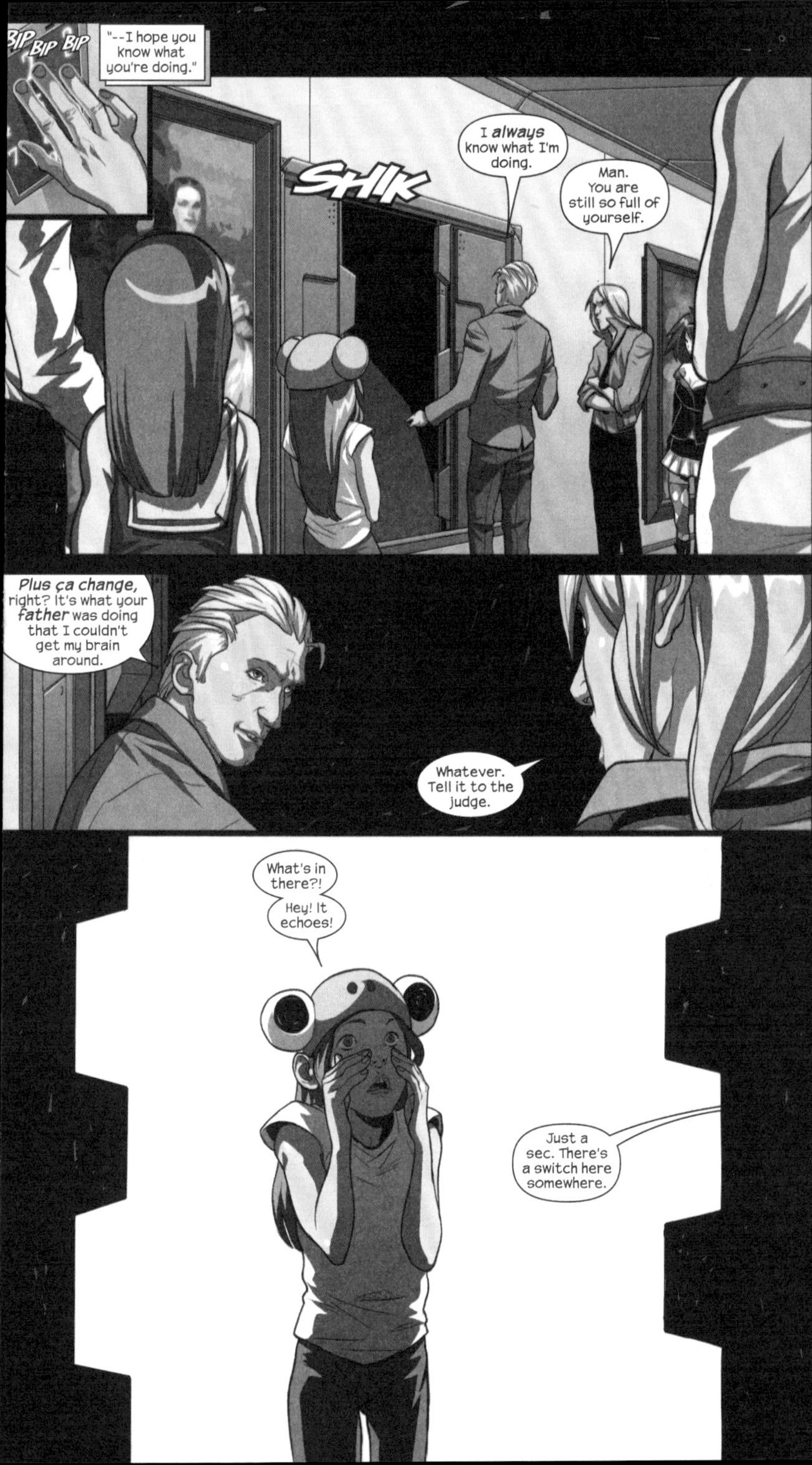
BIP BIP BIP
"--I hope you know what you're doing."
SHIK
I *always* know what I'm doing.
Man. You are still so full of yourself.
Plus ça change, right? It's what your *father* was doing that I couldn't get my brain around.
Whatever. Tell it to the judge.
What's in there?!
Hey! It echoes!
Just a sec. There's a switch here somewhere.

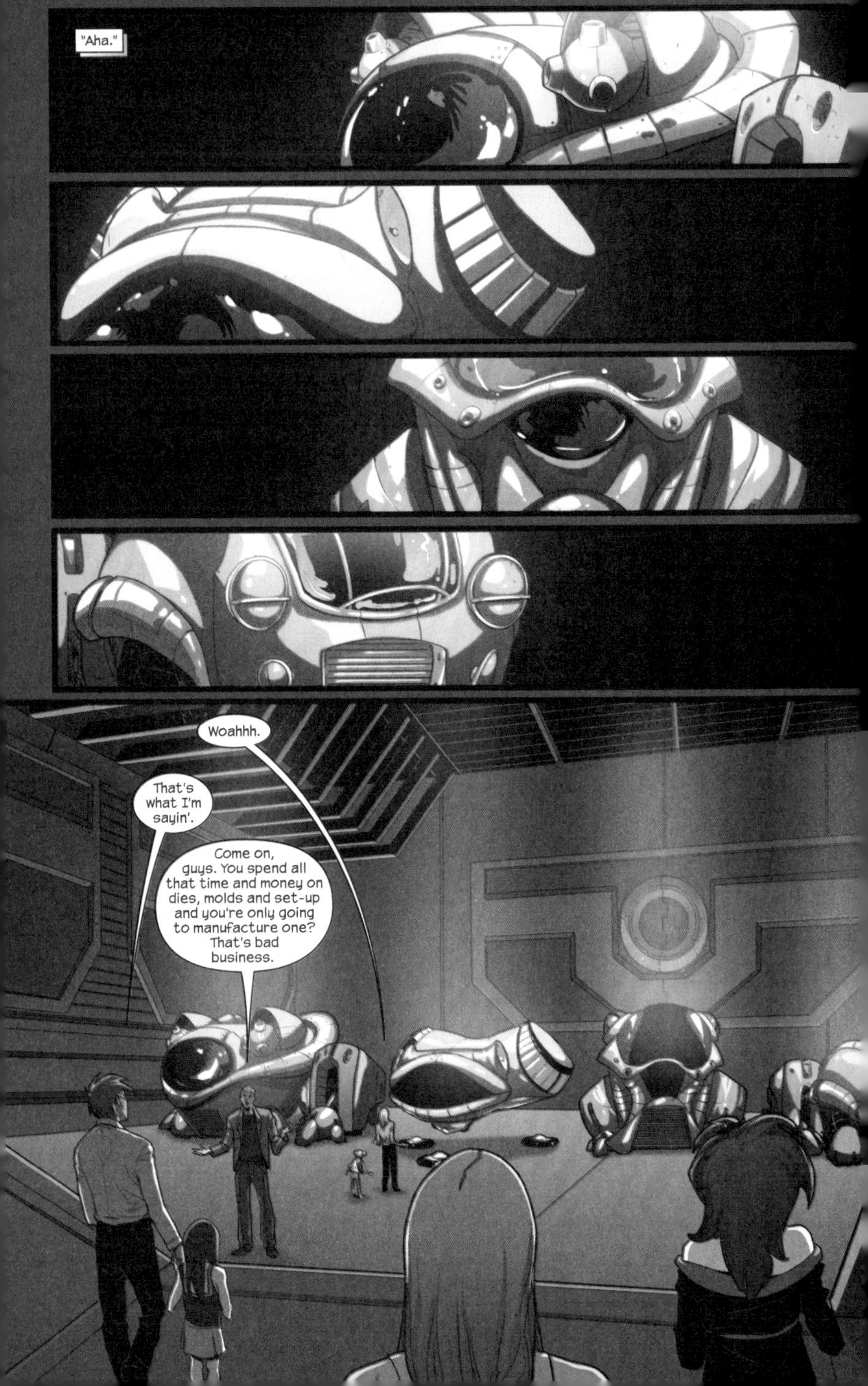
"Aha."
Woahhh.
That's what I'm sayin'.
Come on, guys. You spend all that time and money on dies, molds and set-up and you're only going to manufacture one? That's bad business.

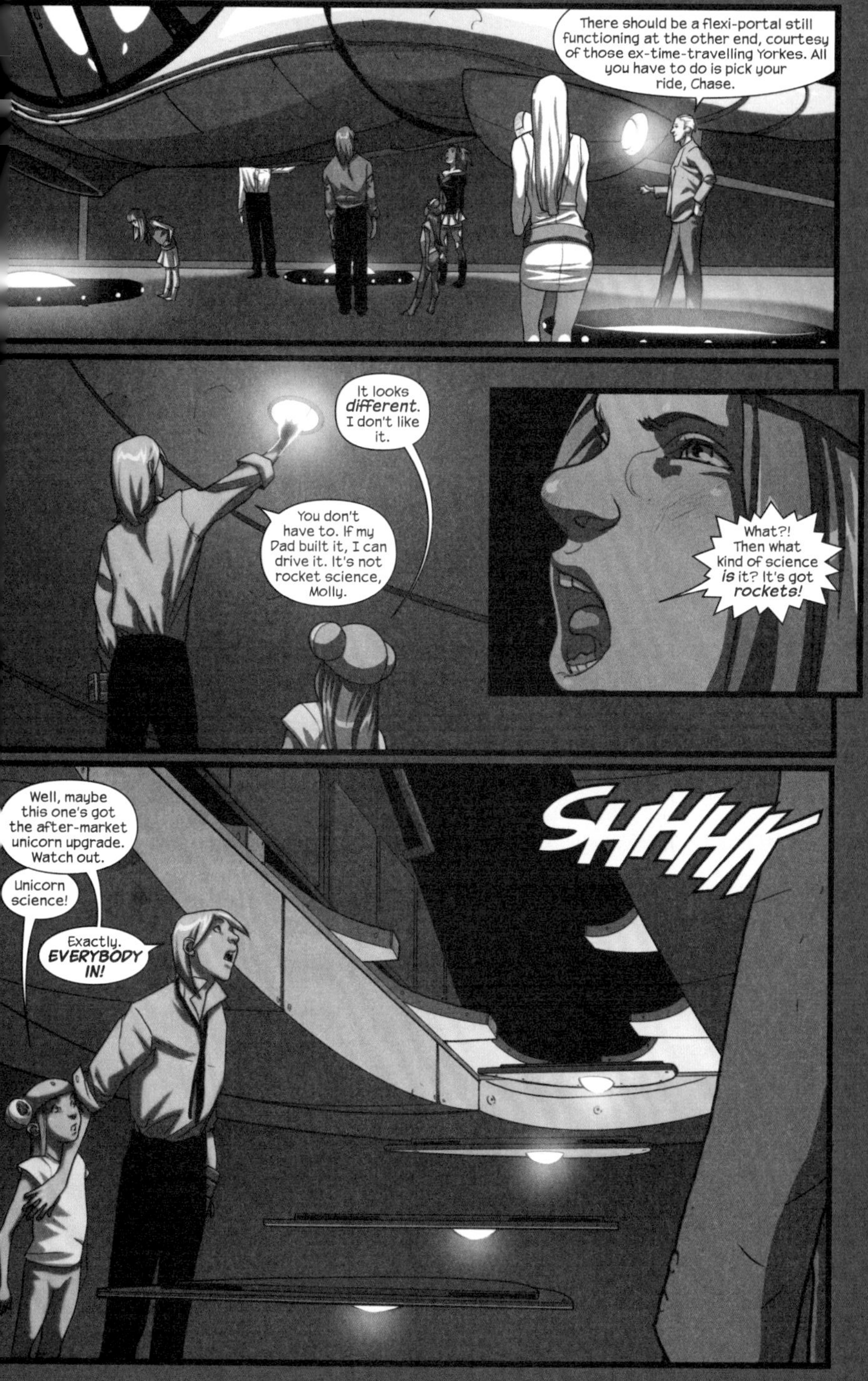
There should be a flexi-portal still functioning at the other end, courtesy of those ex-time-travelling Yorkes. All you have to do is pick your ride, Chase.
It looks *different*. I don't like it.
You don't have to. If my Dad built it, I can drive it. It's not rocket science, Molly.
What?! Then what kind of science *is* it? It's got *rockets!*
Well, maybe this one's got the after-market unicorn upgrade. Watch out.
Unicorn science!
Exactly. **EVERYBODY IN!**
SHHHK

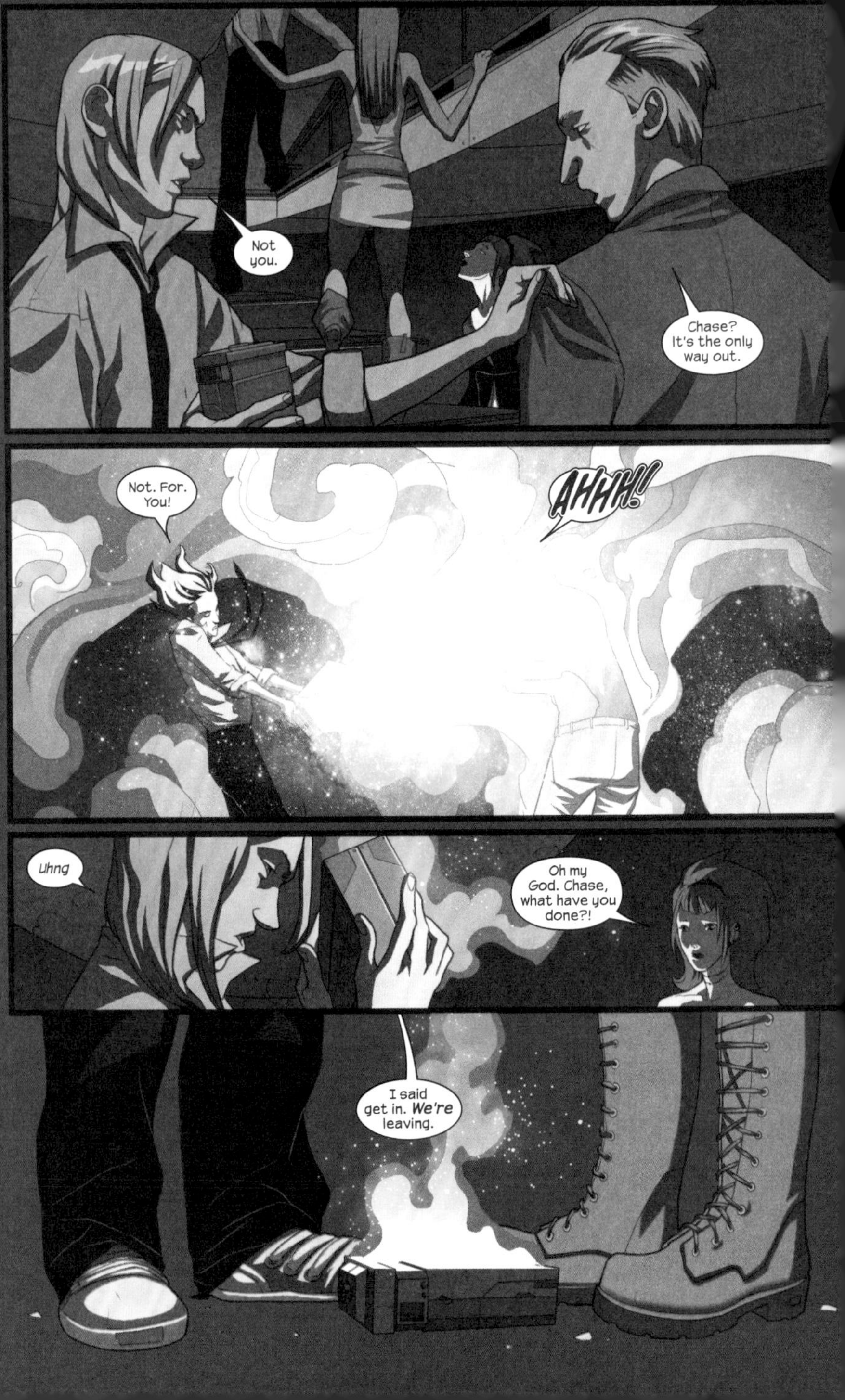
Not you.
Chase? It's the only way out.
Not. For. You!
AHHH!
Uhng
Oh my God. Chase, what have you done?!
I said get in. We're leaving.

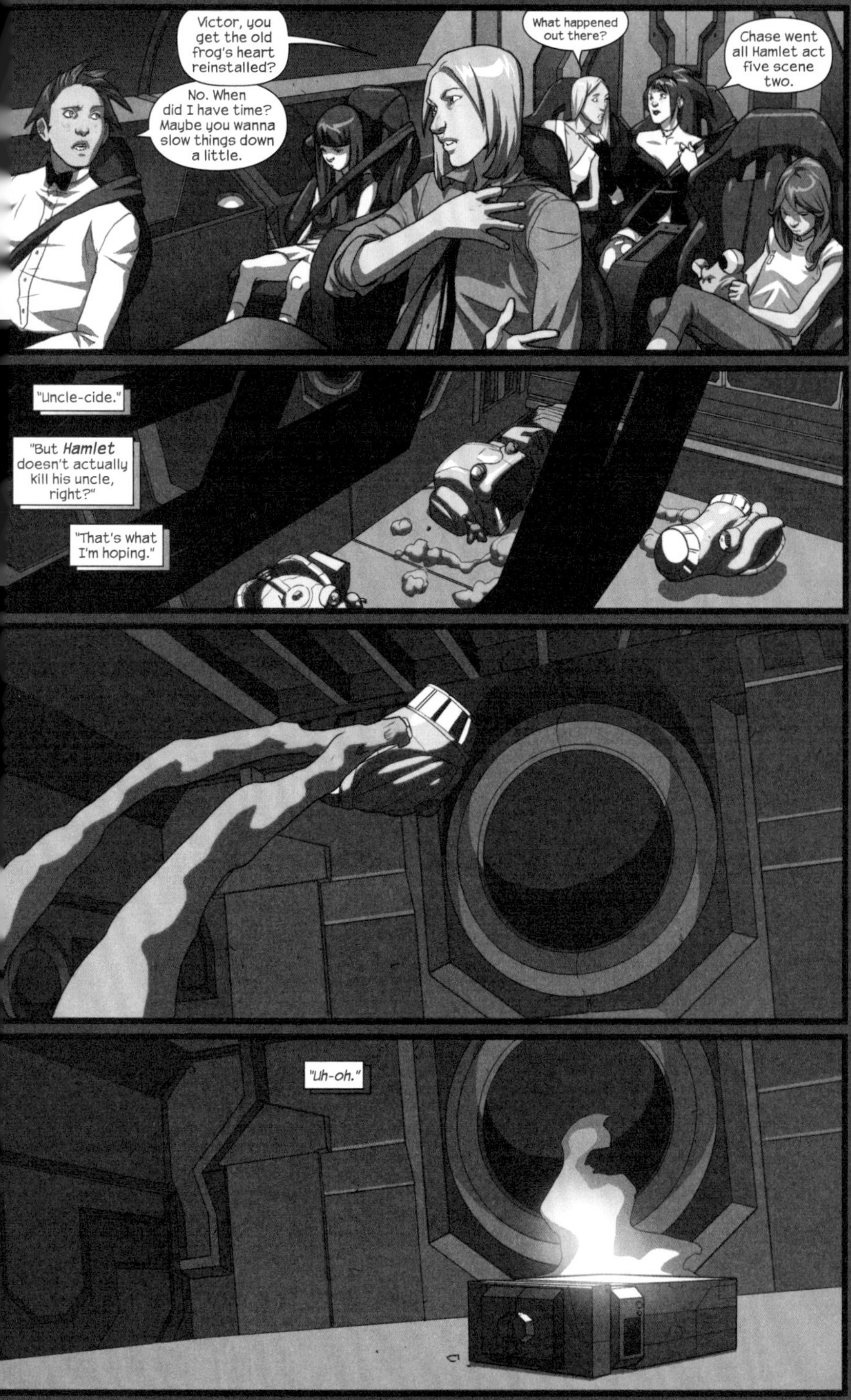
Victor, you get the old frog's heart reinstalled?
No. When did I have time? Maybe you wanna slow things down a little.
What happened out there?
Chase went all Hamlet act five scene two.
"Uncle-cide."
"But *Hamlet* doesn't actually kill his uncle, right?"
"That's what I'm hoping."
"Uh-oh."

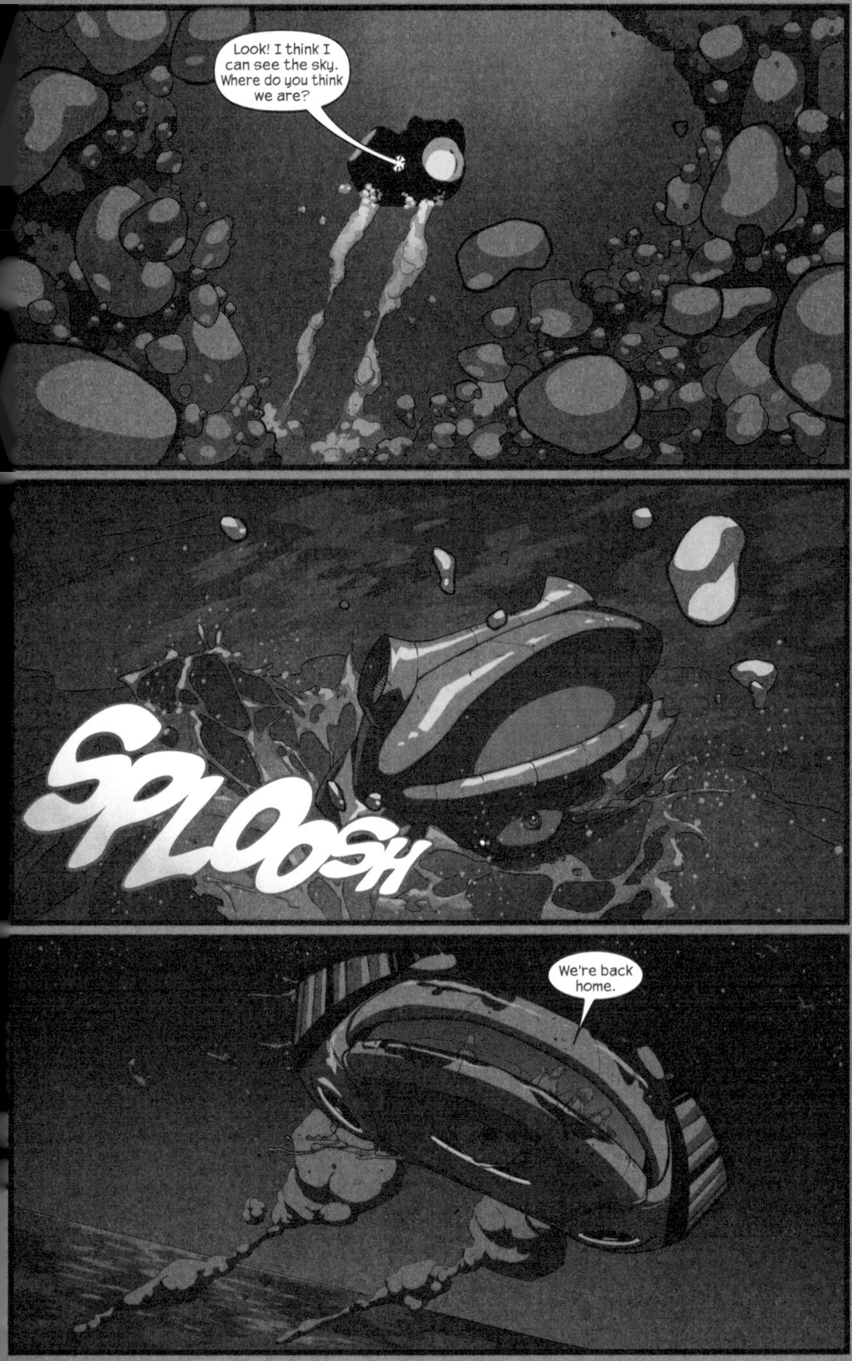
Look! I think I can see the sky. Where do you think we are?
SPLOOSH
We're back home.

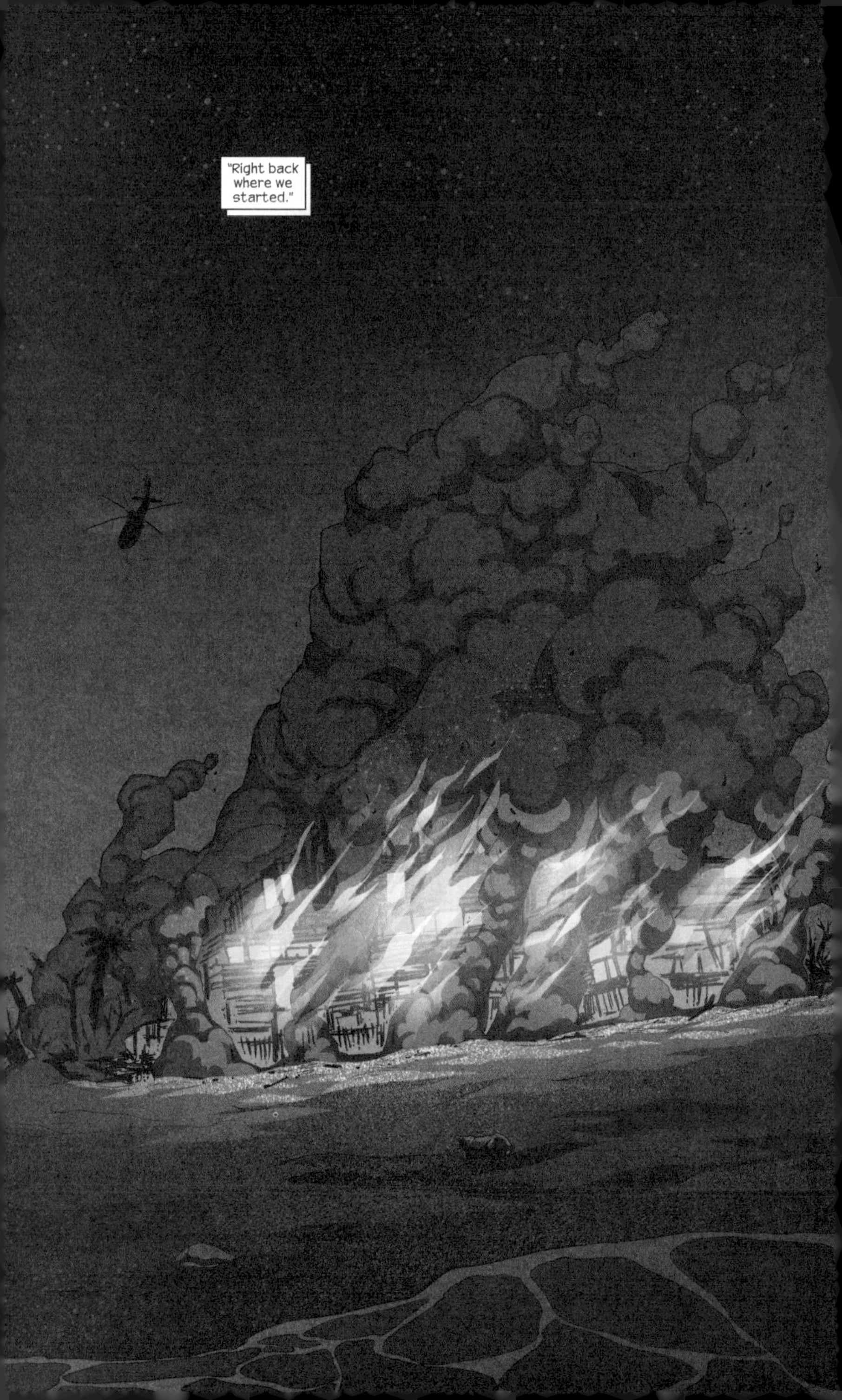
"Right back where we started."

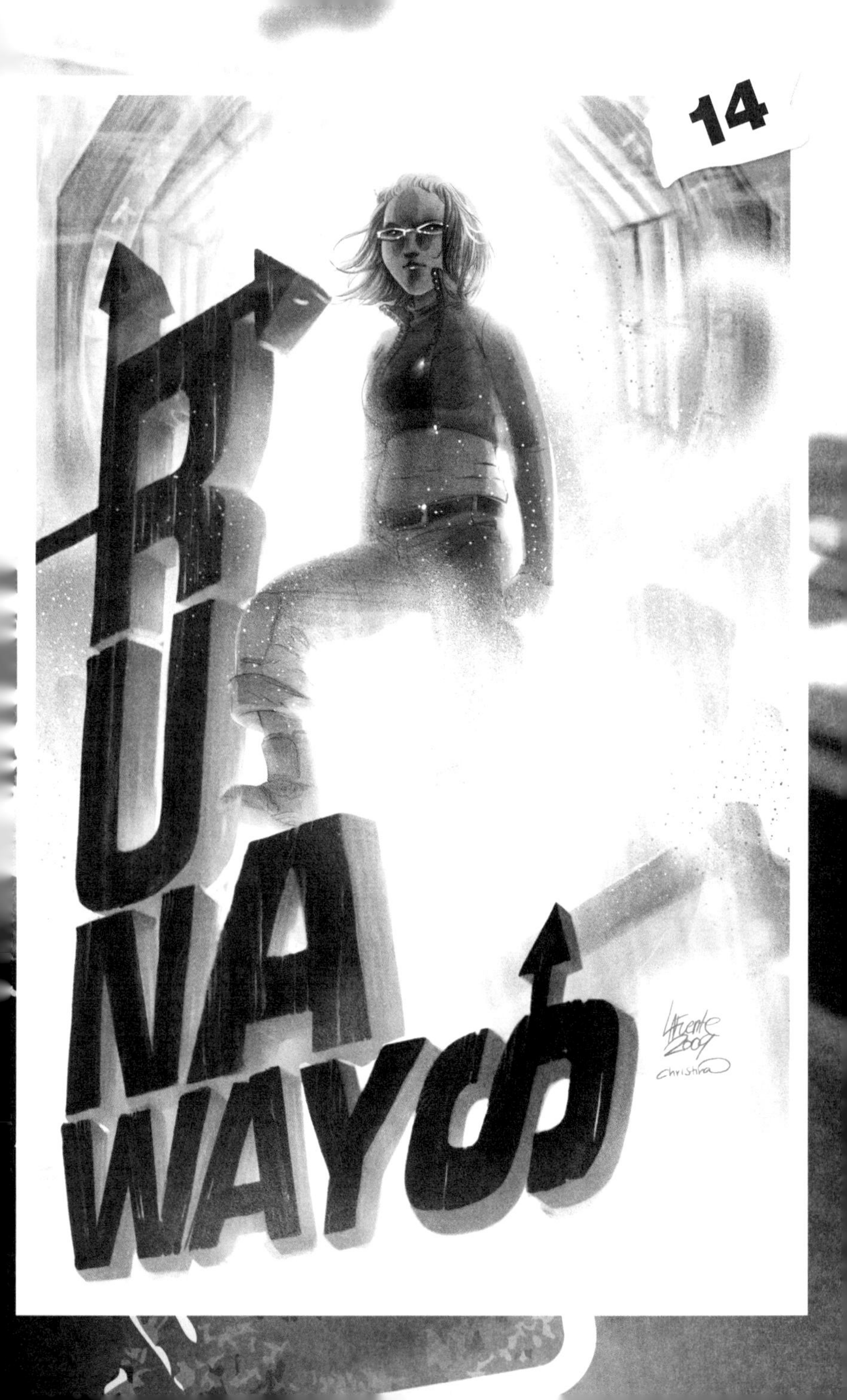
14
RUNAWAYS

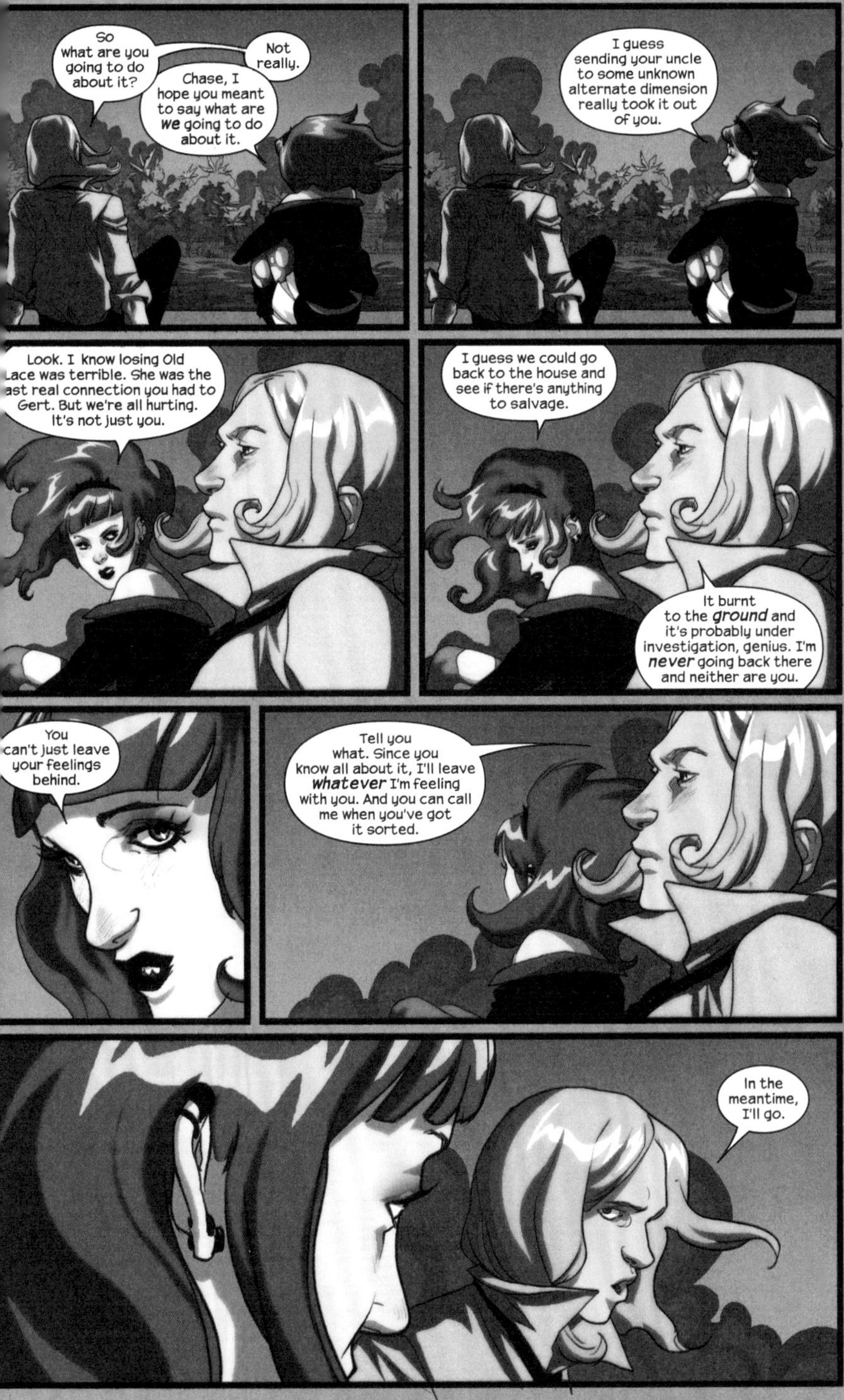
So what are you going to do about it?
Not really.
Chase, I hope you meant to say what are **we** going to do about it.
I guess sending your uncle to some unknown alternate dimension really took it out of you.
Look. I know losing Old Lace was terrible. She was the last real connection you had to Gert. But we're all hurting. It's not just you.
I guess we could go back to the house and see if there's anything to salvage.
It burnt to the **ground** and it's probably under investigation, genius. I'm **never** going back there and neither are you.
You can't just leave your feelings behind.
Tell you what. Since you know all about it, I'll leave **whatever** I'm feeling with you. And you can call me when you've got it sorted.
In the meantime, I'll go.

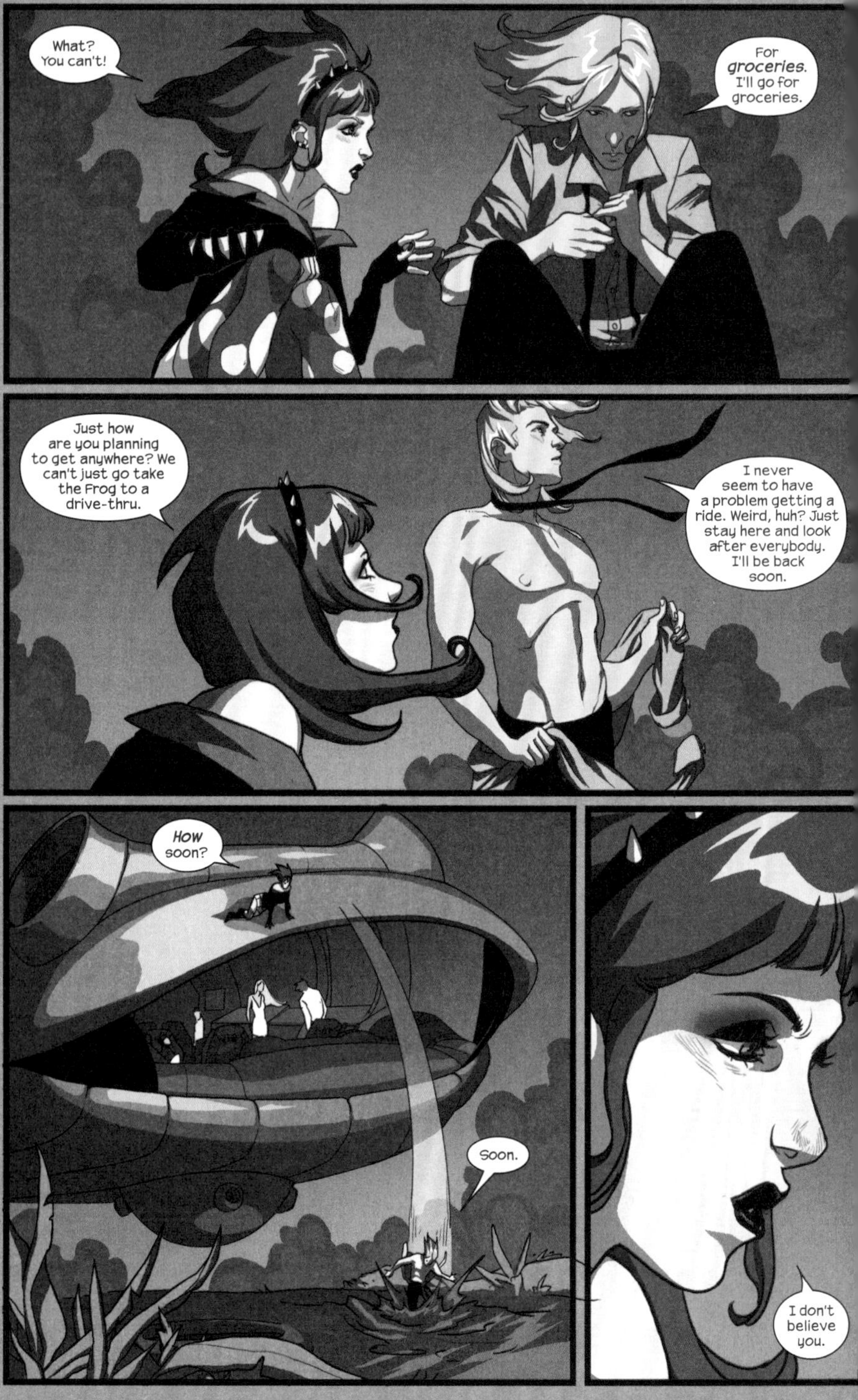
What? You can't!
For groceries. I'll go for groceries.
Just how are you planning to get anywhere? We can't just go take the Frog to a drive-thru.
I never seem to have a problem getting a ride. Weird, huh? Just stay here and look after everybody. I'll be back soon.
How soon?
Soon.
I don't believe you.

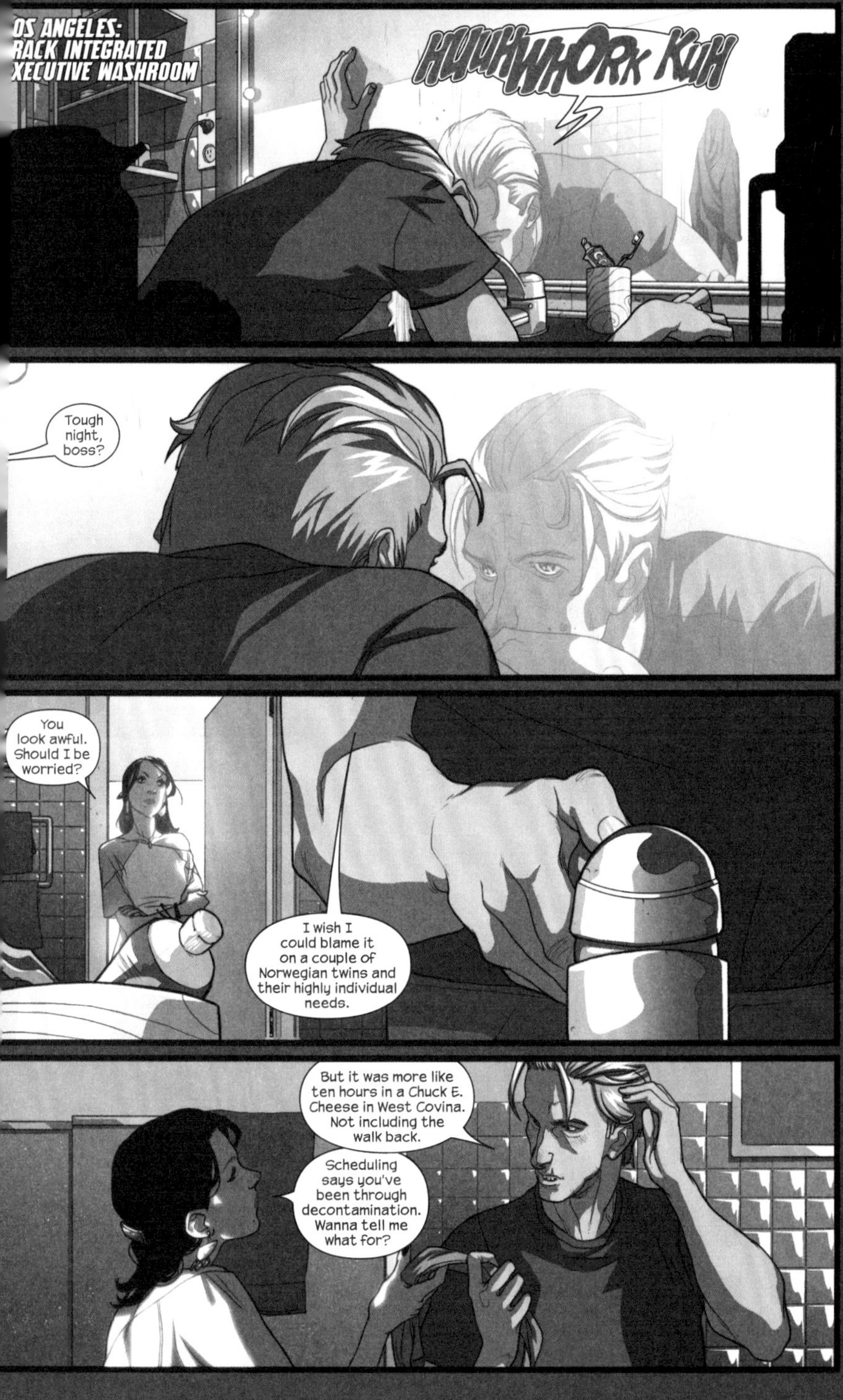

OS ANGELES:
RACK INTEGRATED
XECUTIVE WASHROOM
HUUHWHORK KUH
Tough night, boss?
You look awful. Should I be worried?
I wish I could blame it on a couple of Norwegian twins and their highly individual needs.
But it was more like ten hours in a Chuck E. Cheese in West Covina. Not including the walk back.
Scheduling says you've been through decontamination. Wanna tell me what for?

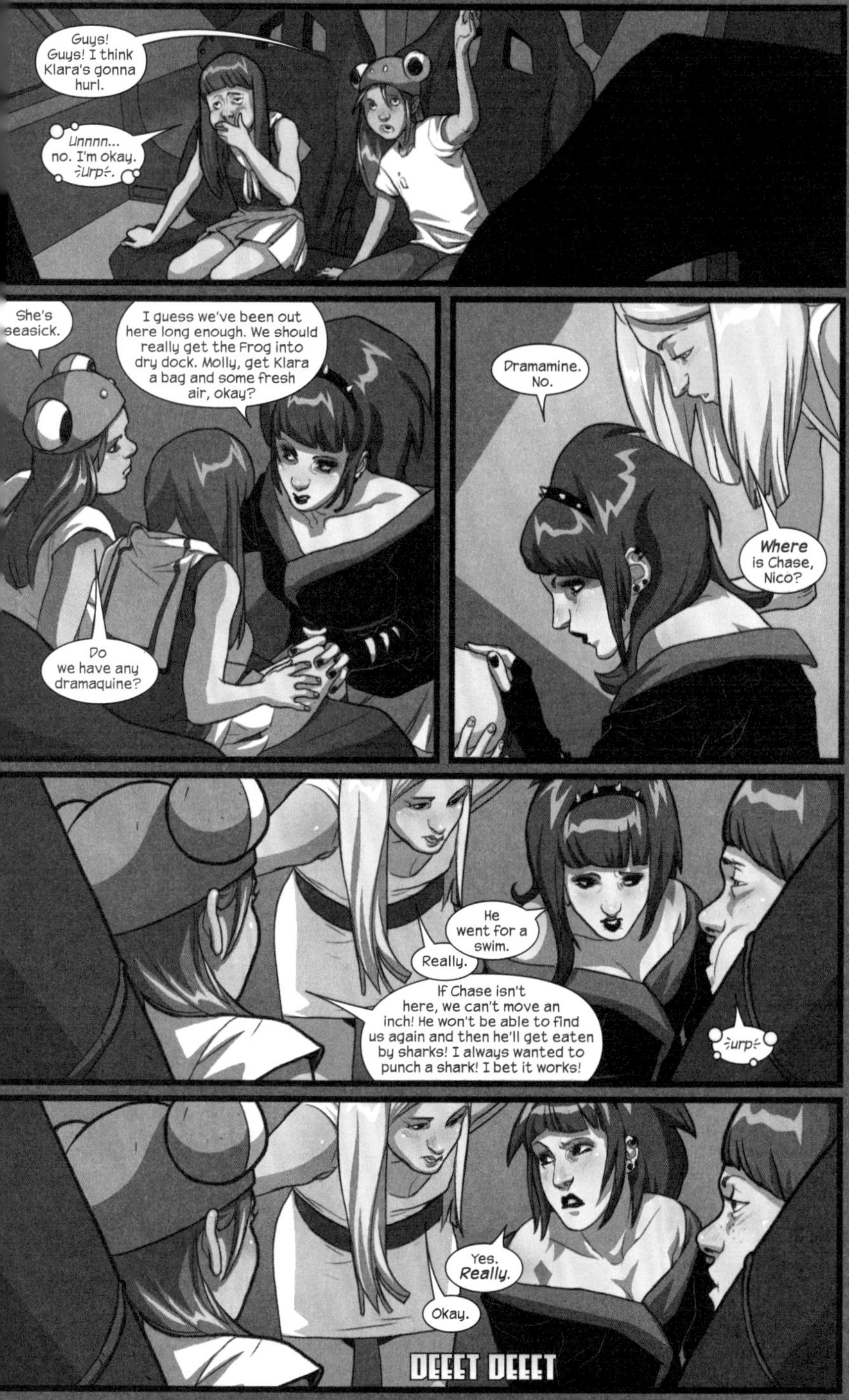
Guys! Guys! I think Klara's gonna hurl.
Unnnn... no. I'm okay. ⁼Urp⁼.
She's seasick.
I guess we've been out here long enough. We should really get the Frog into dry dock. Molly, get Klara a bag and some fresh air, okay?
Do we have any dramaquine?
Dramamine. No.
Where is Chase, Nico?
He went for a swim.
Really.
If Chase isn't here, we can't move an inch! He won't be able to find us again and then he'll get eaten by sharks! I always wanted to punch a shark! I bet it works!
⁼urp⁼
Yes. Really.
Okay.
DEEET DEEET

DEEET
DEEET

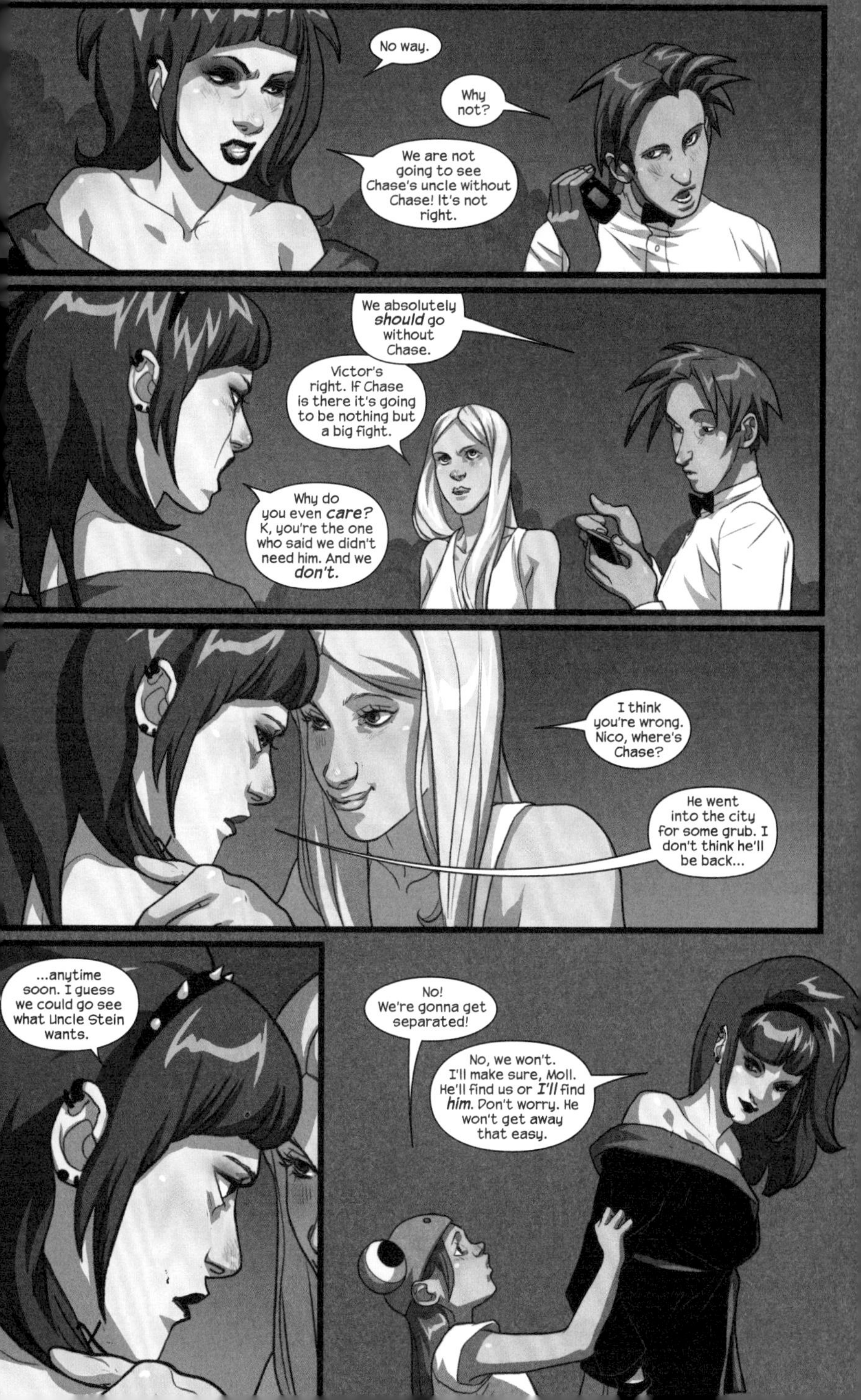

No way.
Why not?
We are not going to see Chase's uncle without Chase! It's not right.
We absolutely *should* go without Chase.
Victor's right. If Chase is there it's going to be nothing but a big fight.
Why do you even *care?* K, you're the one who said we didn't need him. And we *don't.*
I think you're wrong. Nico, where's Chase?
He went into the city for some grub. I don't think he'll be back...
...anytime soon. I guess we could go see what Uncle Stein wants.
No! We're gonna get separated!
No, we won't. I'll make sure, Moll. He'll find us or *I'll* find *him*. Don't worry. He won't get away that easy.

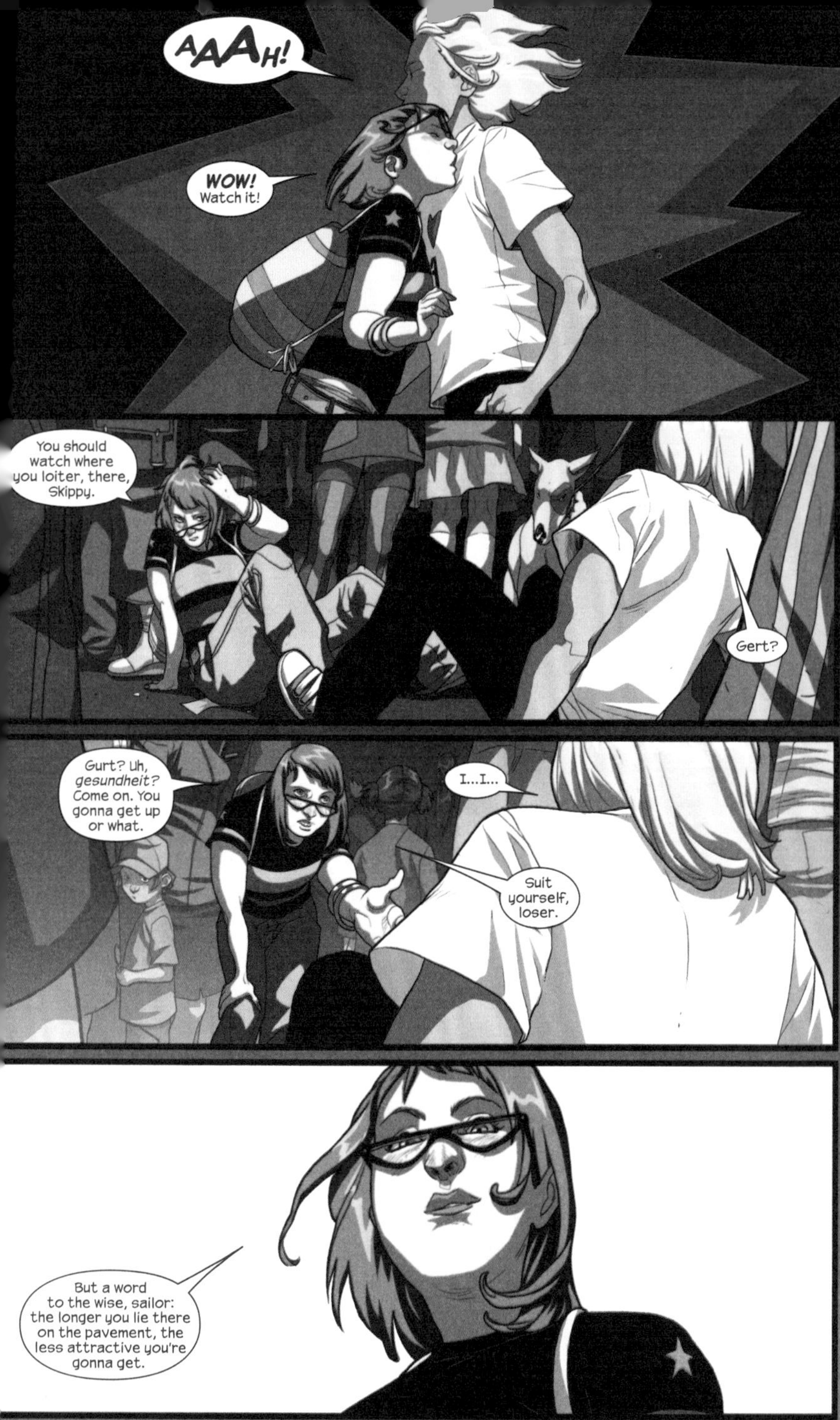
AAAH!
WOW! Watch it!
You should watch where you loiter, there, Skippy.
Gert?
Gurt? Uh, *gesundheit?* Come on. You gonna get up or what.
I...I...
Suit yourself, loser.
But a word to the wise, sailor: the longer you lie there on the pavement, the less attractive you're gonna get.

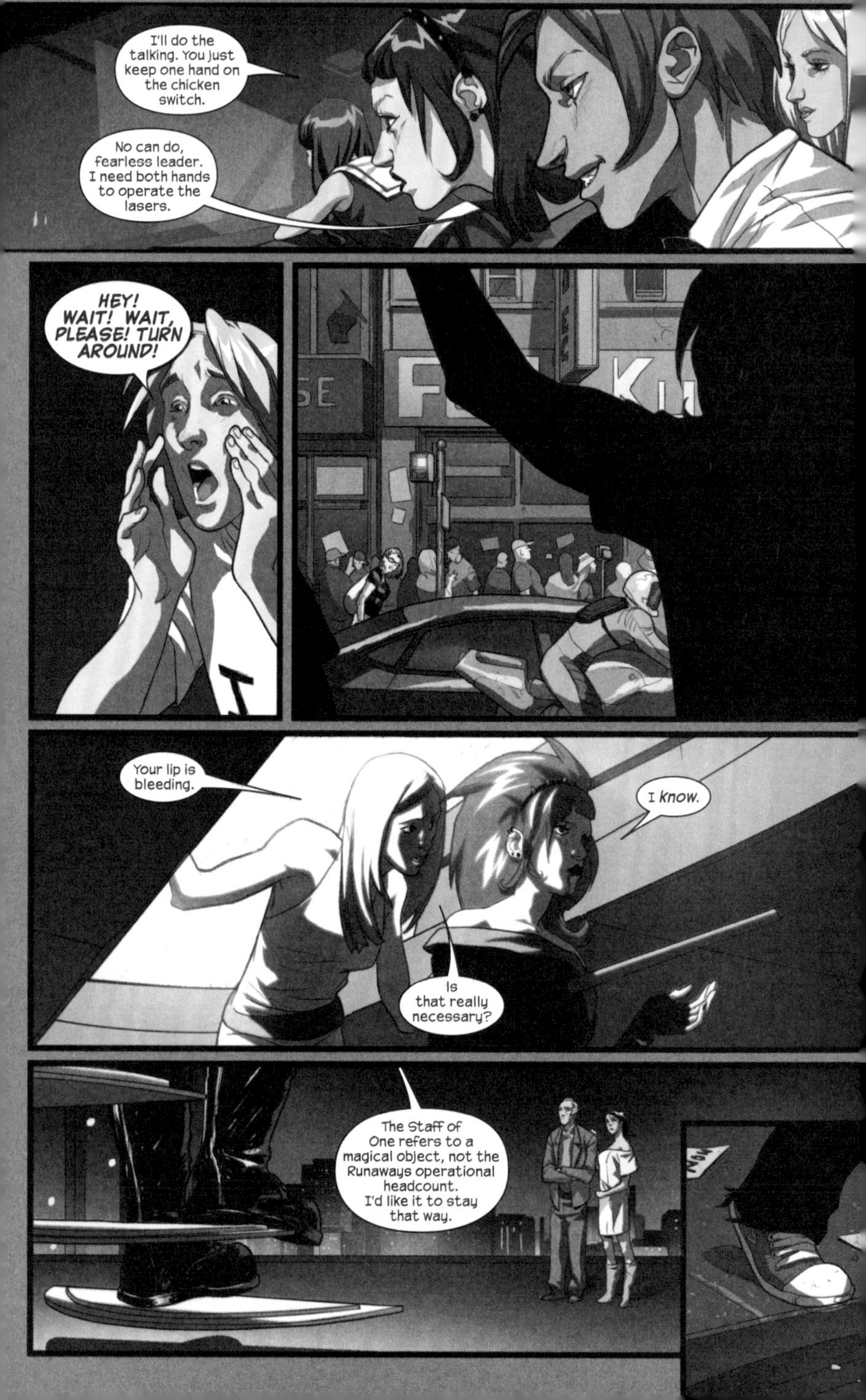

I'll do the talking. You just keep one hand on the chicken switch.
No can do, fearless leader. I need both hands to operate the lasers.
HEY! WAIT! WAIT, PLEASE! TURN AROUND!
Your lip is bleeding.
I know.
Is that really necessary?
The Staff of One refers to a magical object, not the Runaways operational headcount. I'd like it to stay that way.

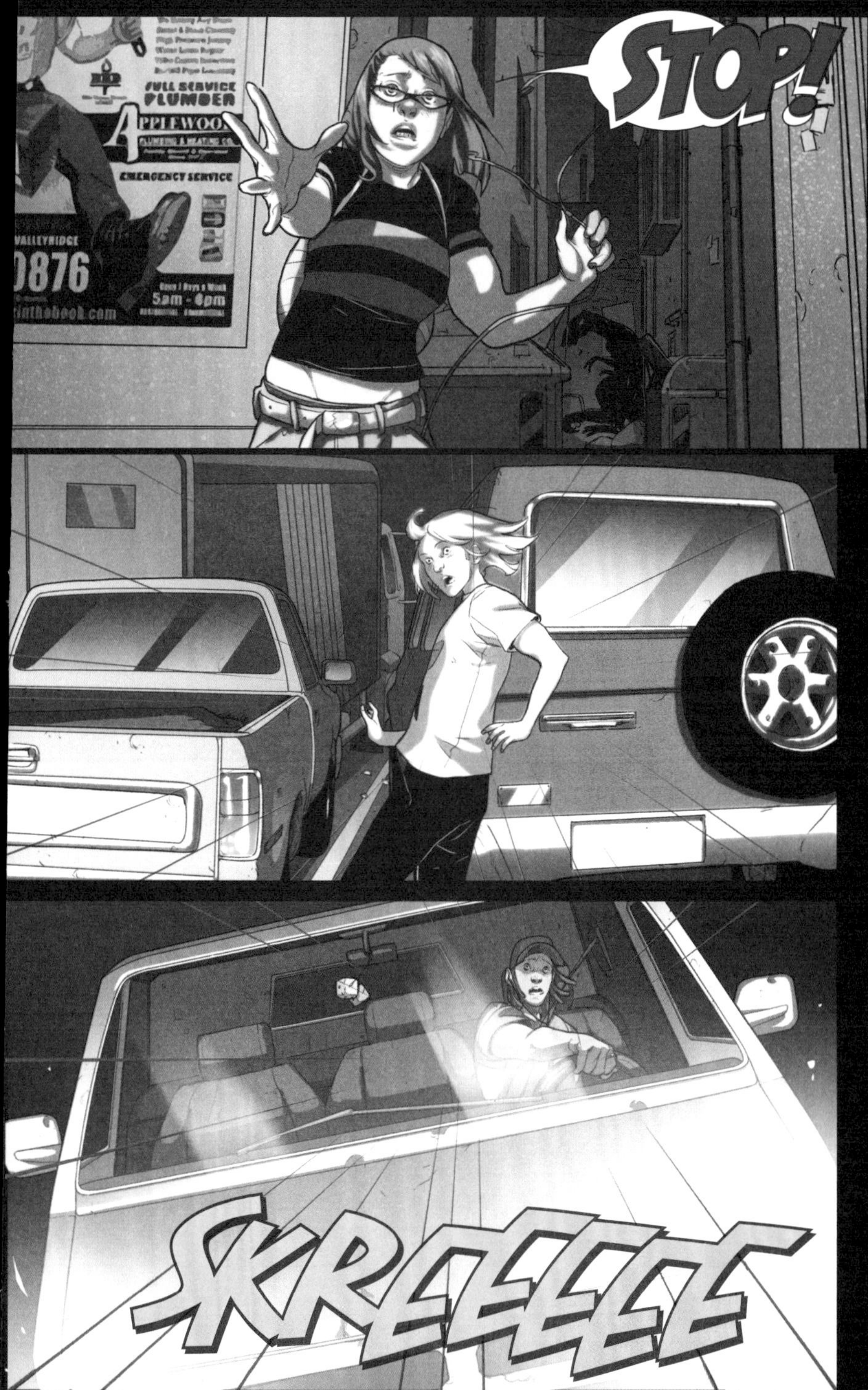
STOP!
FULL SERVICE PLUMBER
EMERGENCY SERVICE
0876
5am - 6pm
SKREEEEE

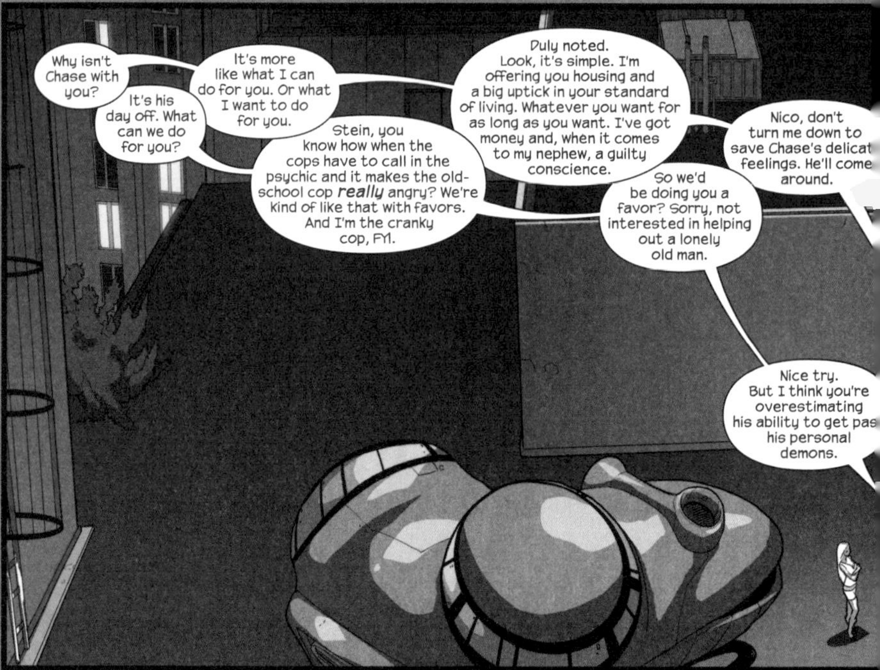
Why isn't Chase with you?
It's his day off. What can we do for you?
It's more like what I can do for you. Or what I want to do for you.
Stein, you know how when the cops have to call in the psychic and it makes the old-school cop *really* angry? We're kind of like that with favors. And I'm the cranky cop, FYI.
Duly noted. Look, it's simple. I'm offering you housing and a big uptick in your standard of living. Whatever you want for as long as you want. I've got money and, when it comes to my nephew, a guilty conscience.
So we'd be doing you a favor? Sorry, not interested in helping out a lonely old man.
Nico, don't turn me down to save Chase's delicat feelings. He'll come around.
Nice try. But I think you're overestimating his ability to get pas his personal demons.

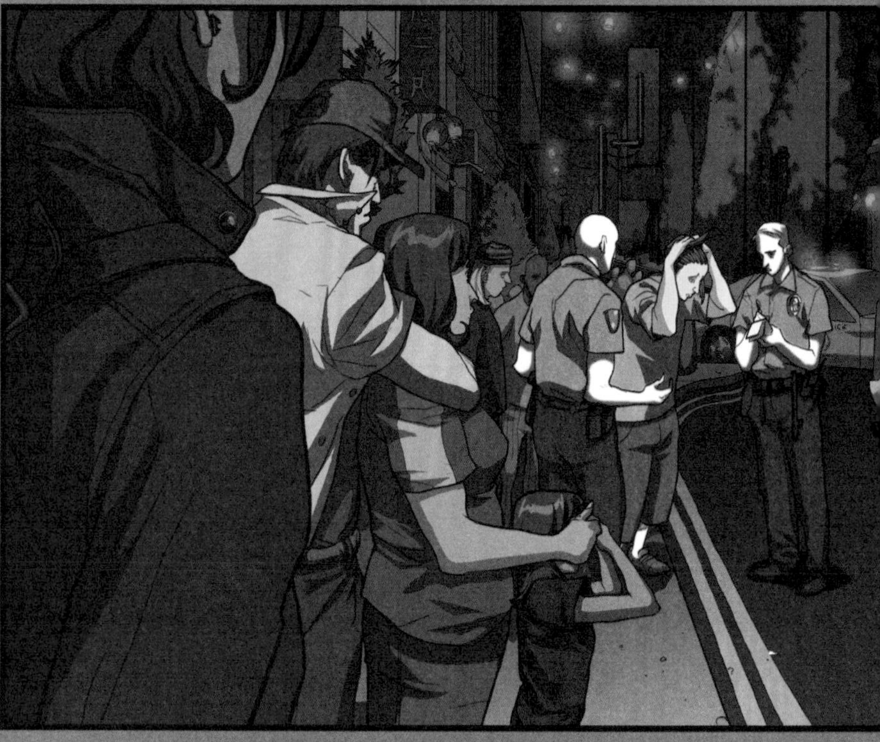

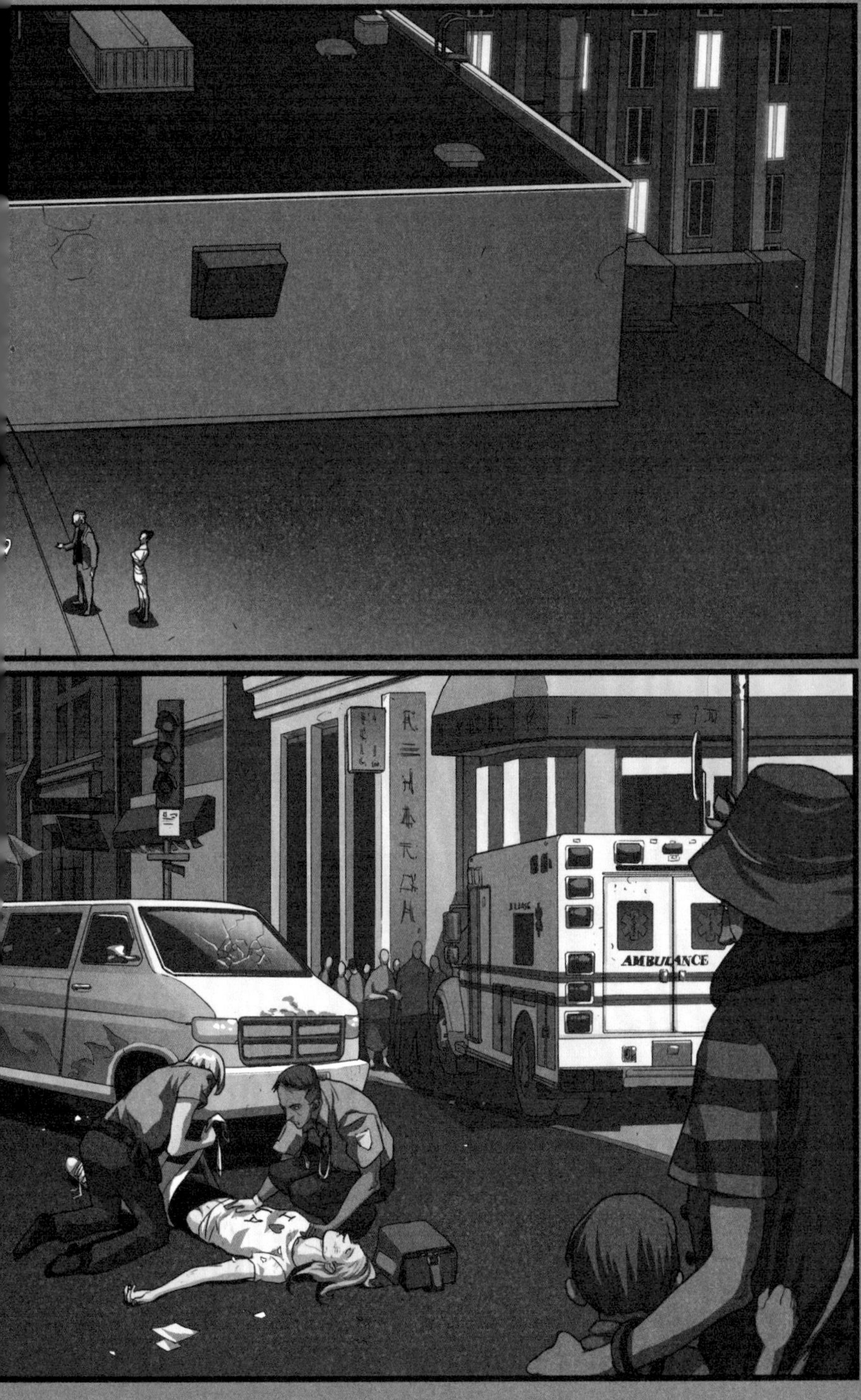
AMBULANCE

And we've got all of this.

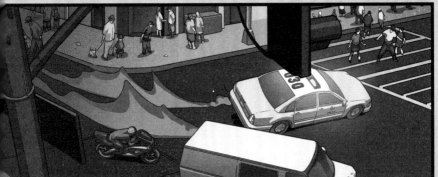

EMERGENC
ROOM

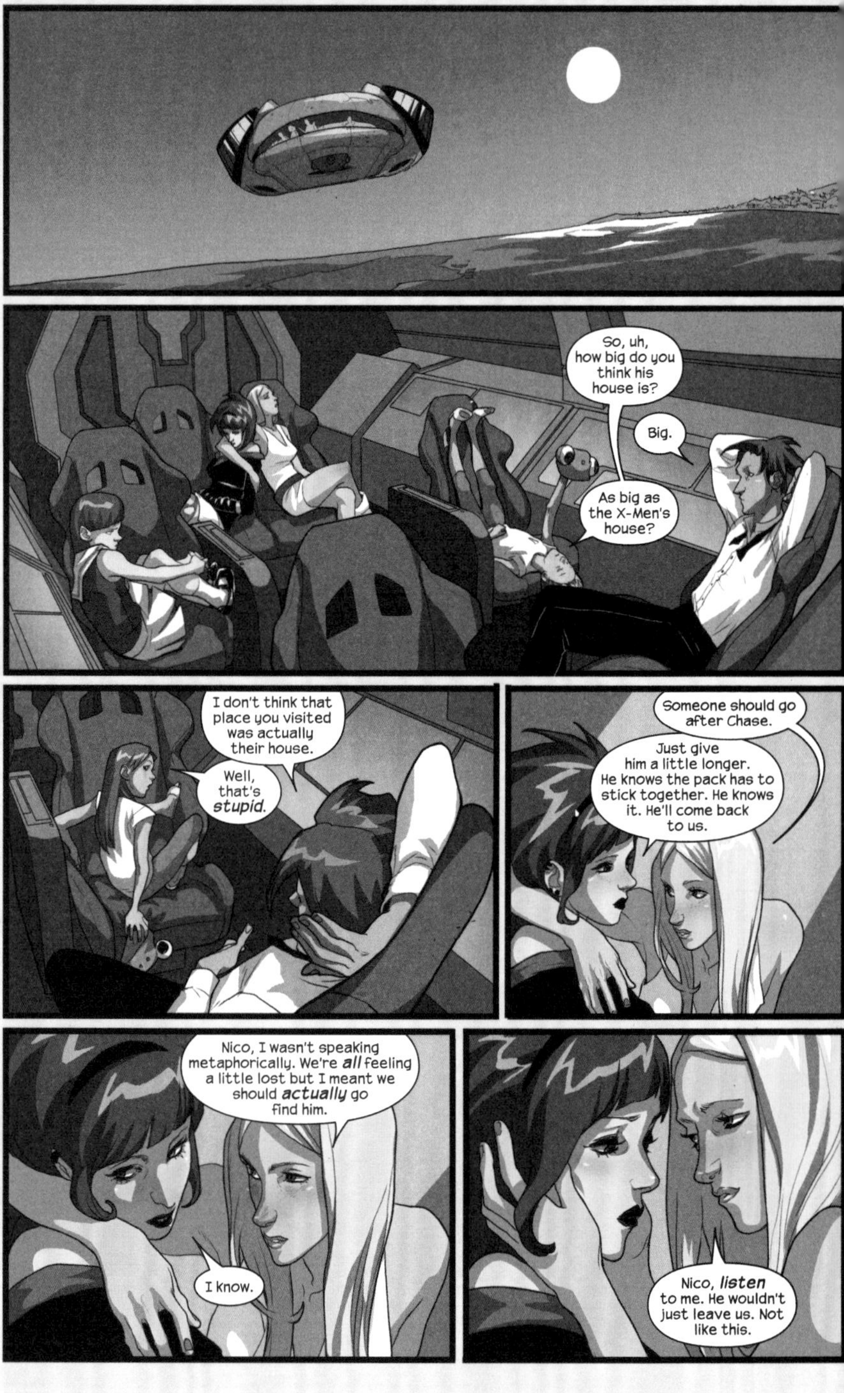
So, uh, how big do you think his house is?
Big.
As big as the X-Men's house?
I don't think that place you visited was actually their house.
Well, that's *stupid*.
Someone should go after Chase.
Just give him a little longer. He knows the pack has to stick together. He knows it. He'll come back to us.
Nico, I wasn't speaking metaphorically. We're *all* feeling a little lost but I meant we should *actually* go find him.
I know.
Nico, *listen* to me. He wouldn't just leave us. Not like this.

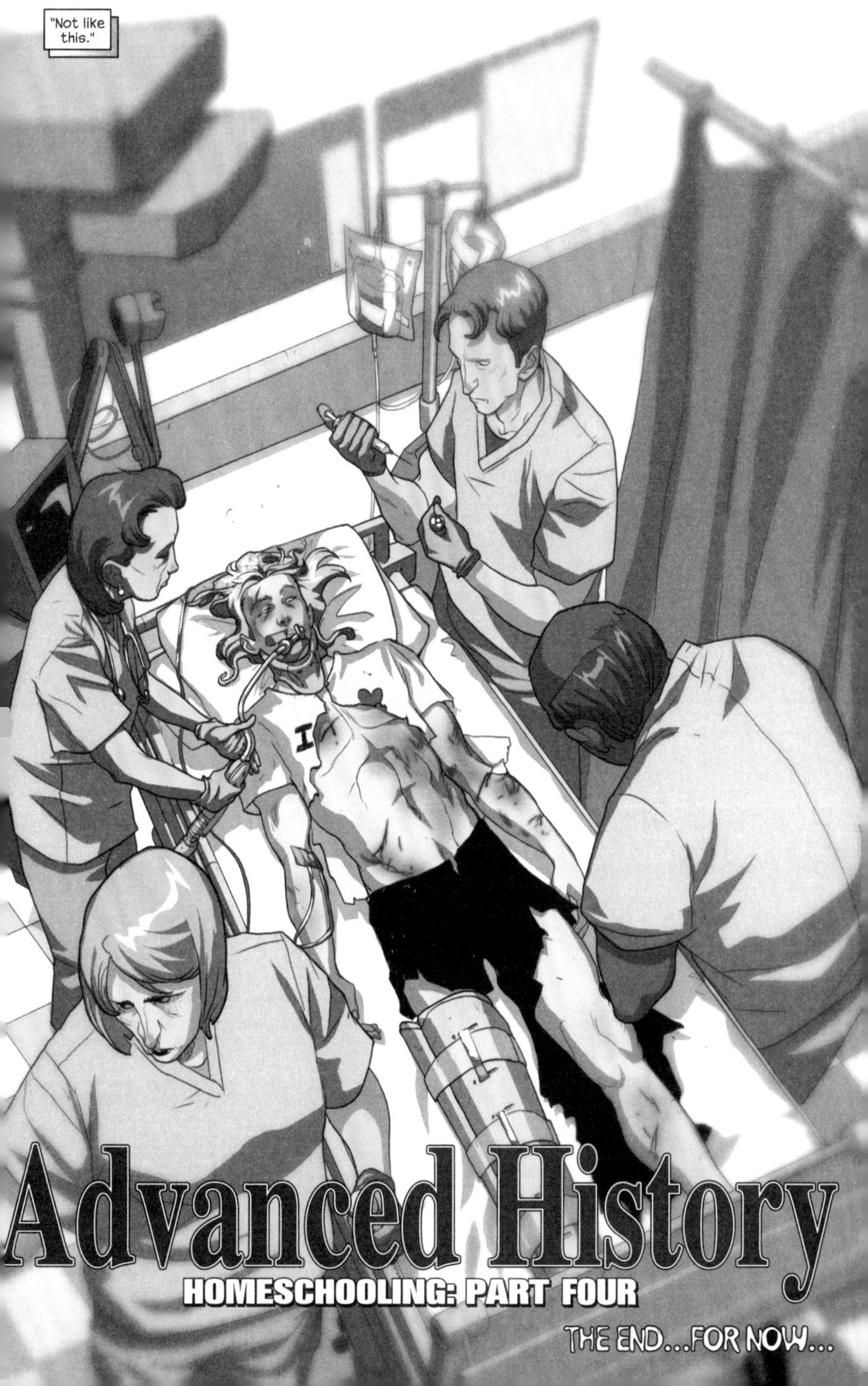
"Not like this."
Advanced History
HOMESCHOOLING: PART FOUR
THE END...FOR NOW...

70TH ANNIVERSARY FRAME VARIANT BY **TAKESHI MIYAZAWA**

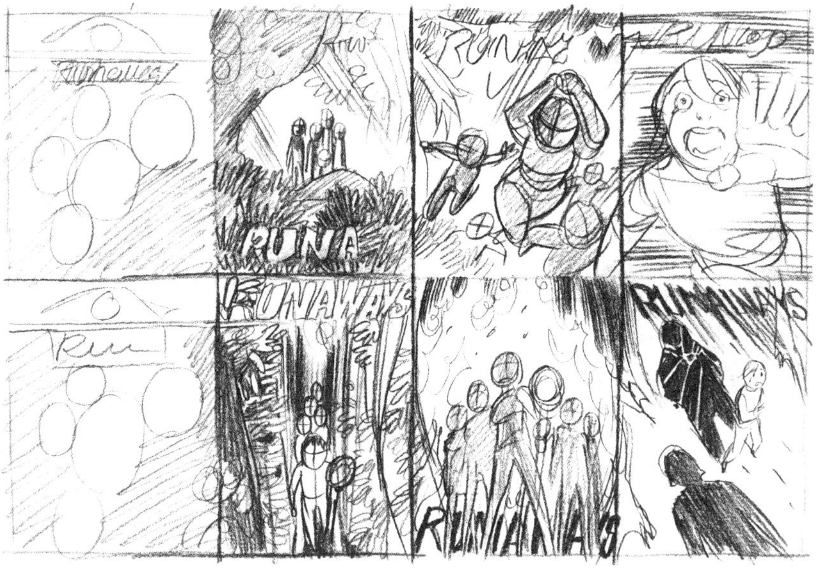
RUNA
RUNAWAYS
RUNAWAYS

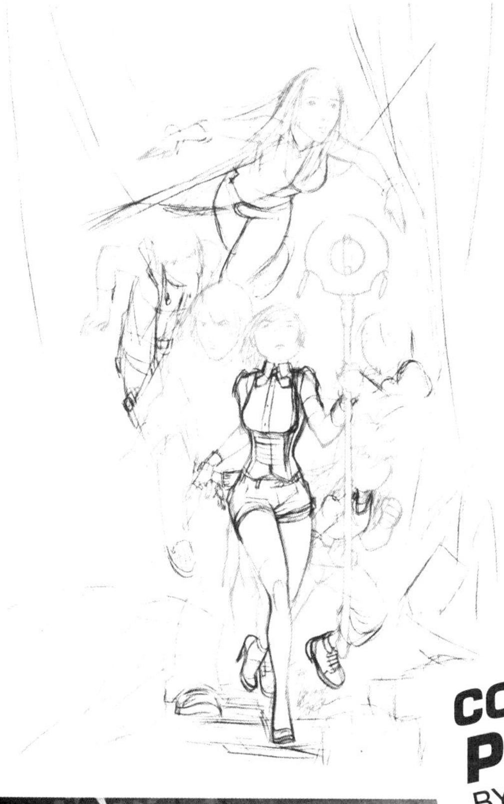

COVER #11-14
PROCESS
BY DAVID LAFUENTE

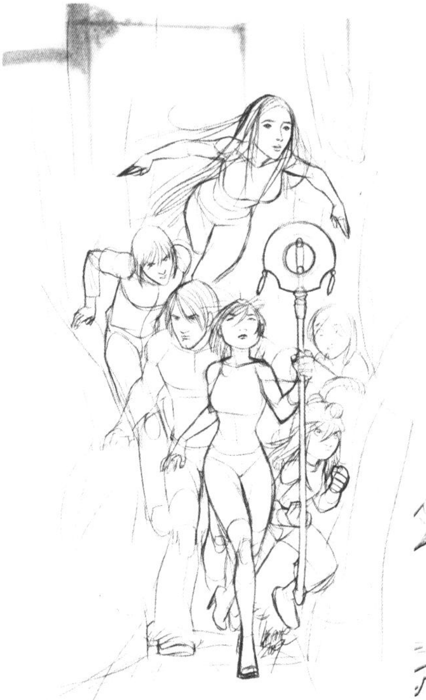

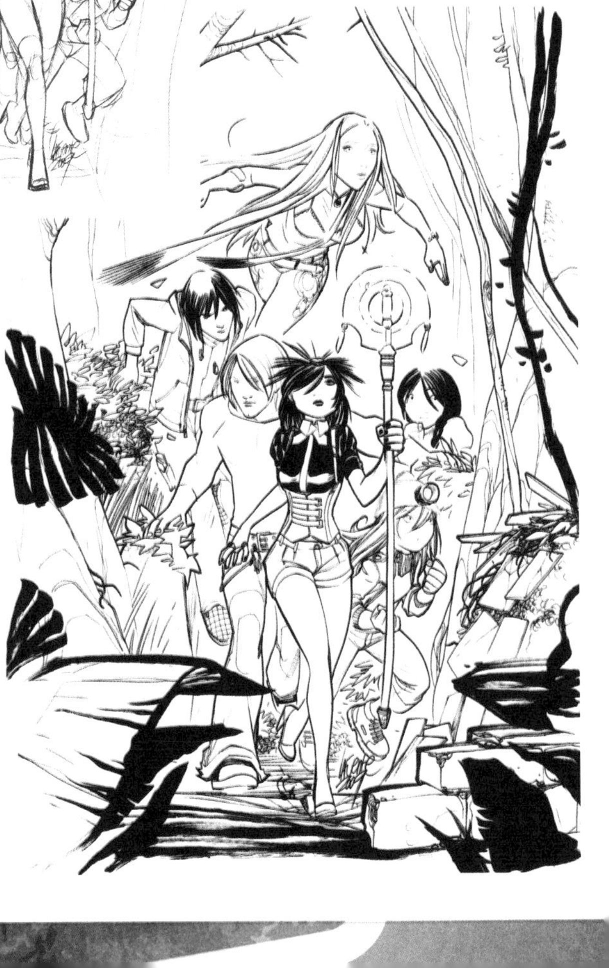

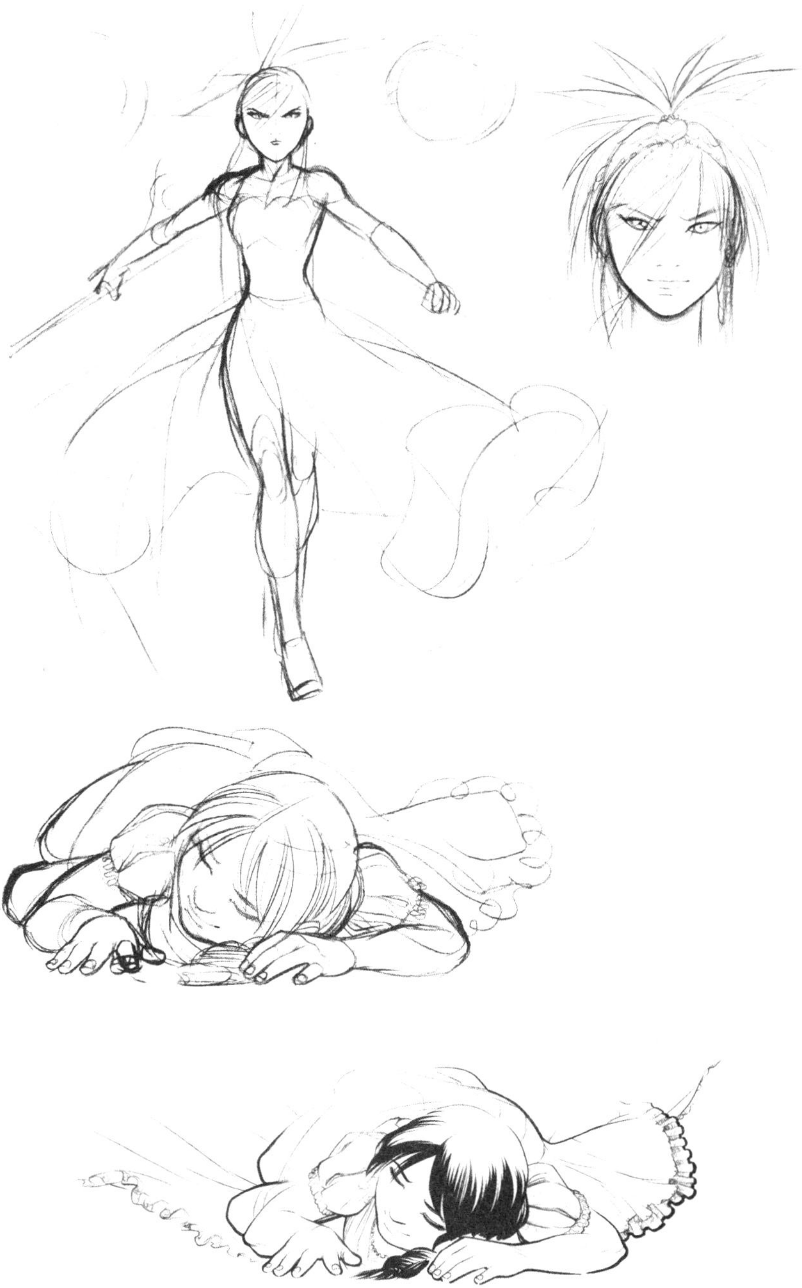

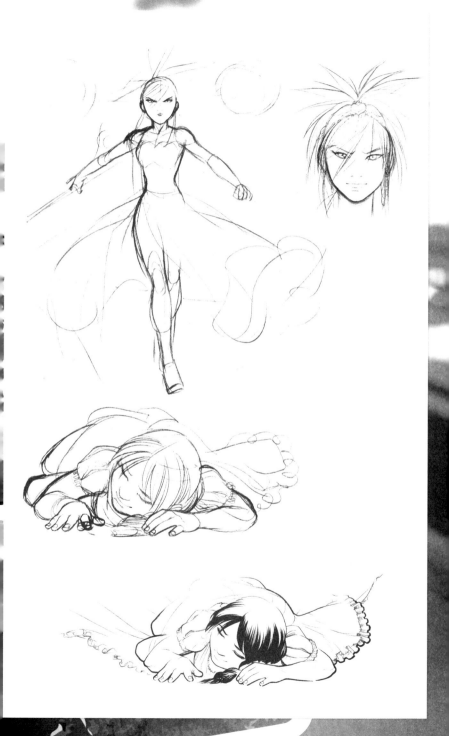

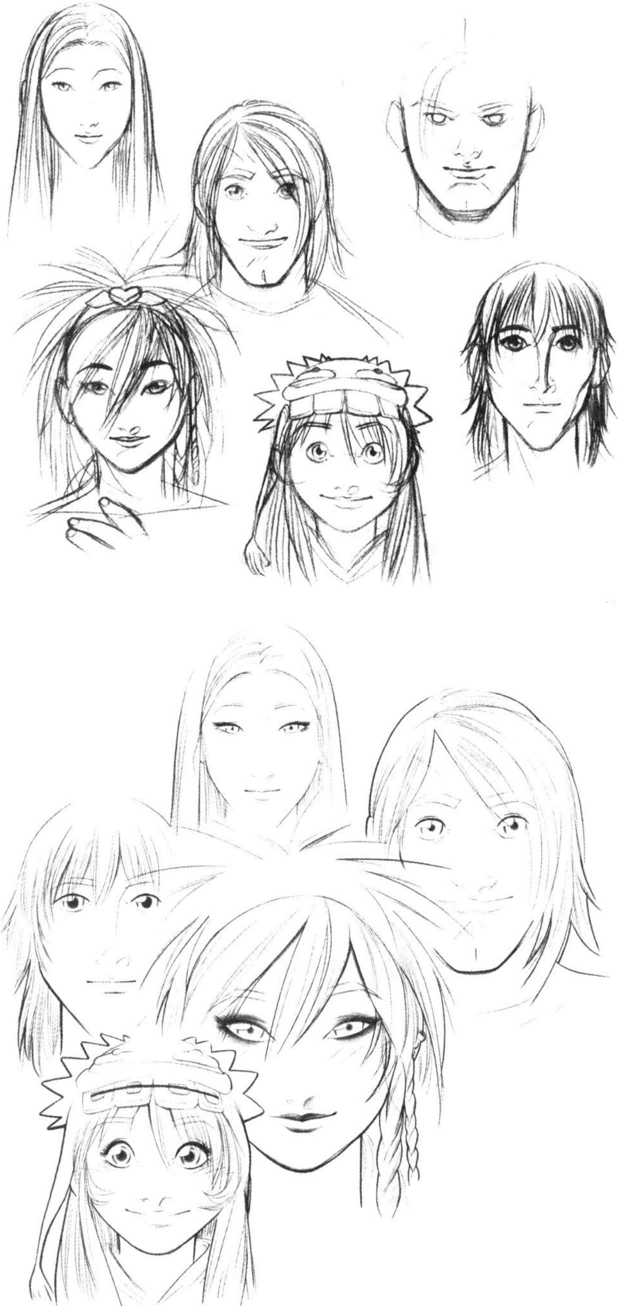

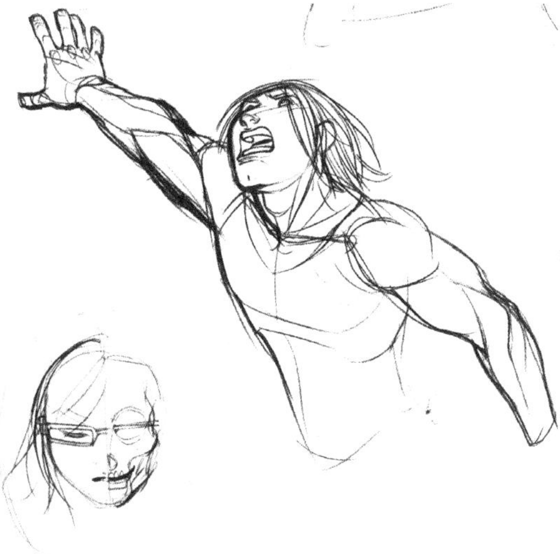

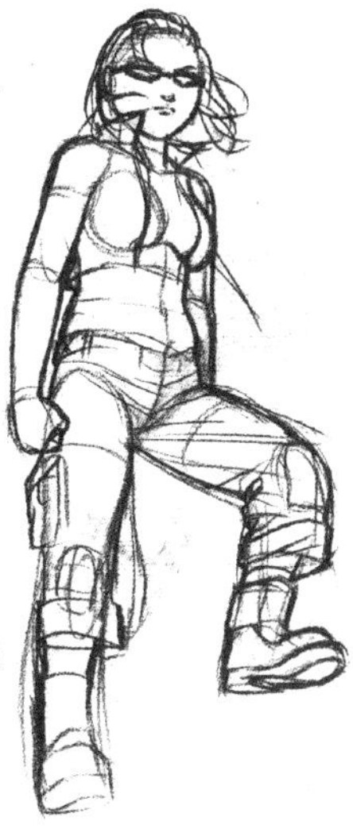

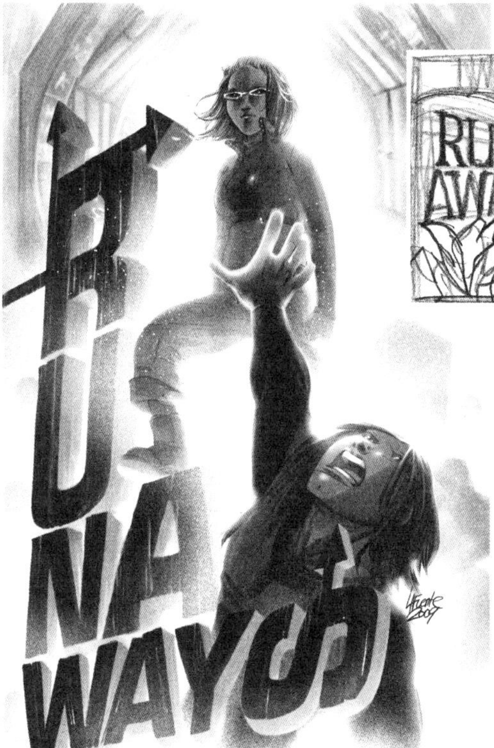
RUNAWAYS

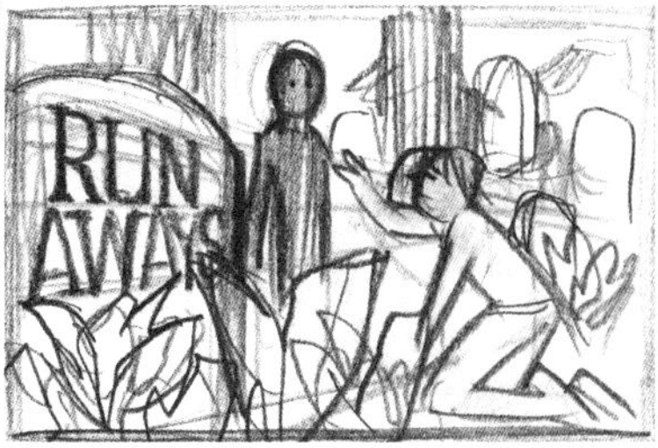
RUN
AWAYS

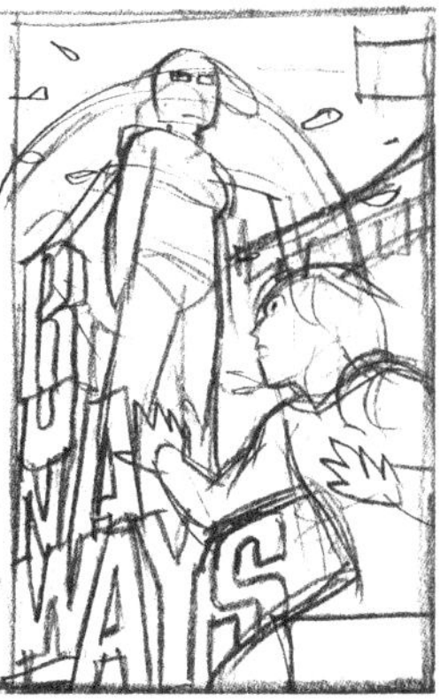
WAYS

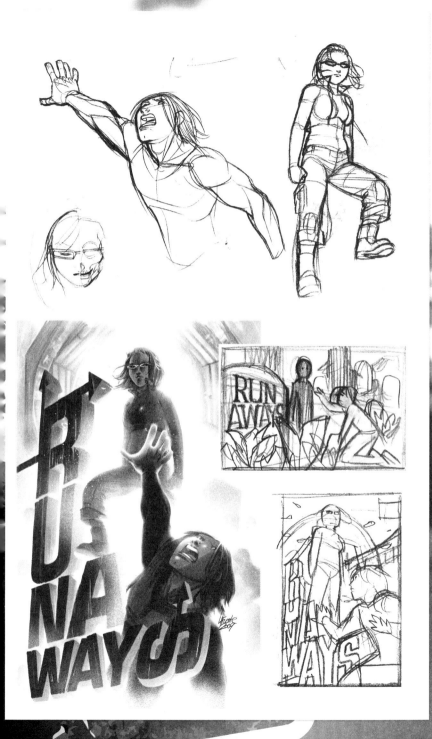

YOUNG AVENGERS

Assembled by Iron Lad (a teenaged version of the time-traveling conqueror known as Kang) Patriot, Hawkeye, Wiccan, Hulkling, Stature, Speed and the Vision are the Young Avengers, following in the footsteps of Earth's mightiest heroes!

WICCAN **HAWKEYE** **VISION** **PATRIOT** **SPEED** **STATURE**

RUNAWAYS

At some point in their lives, all kids think their parents are evil. For Molly Hayes and her friends, this is especially true, as they discover their parents are in fact a group of super-powered crime bosses called "The Pride". Using technology and resources stolen from their parents, the teens break The Pride's criminal hold on Los Angeles. But they've been on the run ever since.

MOLLY HAYES **GERT STEIN** **KAROLINA DEAN** **VICTOR MANCHA** **NICO MINORU** **ALEX WILDER** **CHASE STEIN**

These two teams of super-powered teens have crossed paths before in troubled times, but what if fate proposed a different path for the fledgling heroes? What if their destinies were intertwined in ways they could never be prepared for? What if... the Runaways became the Young Avengers?!

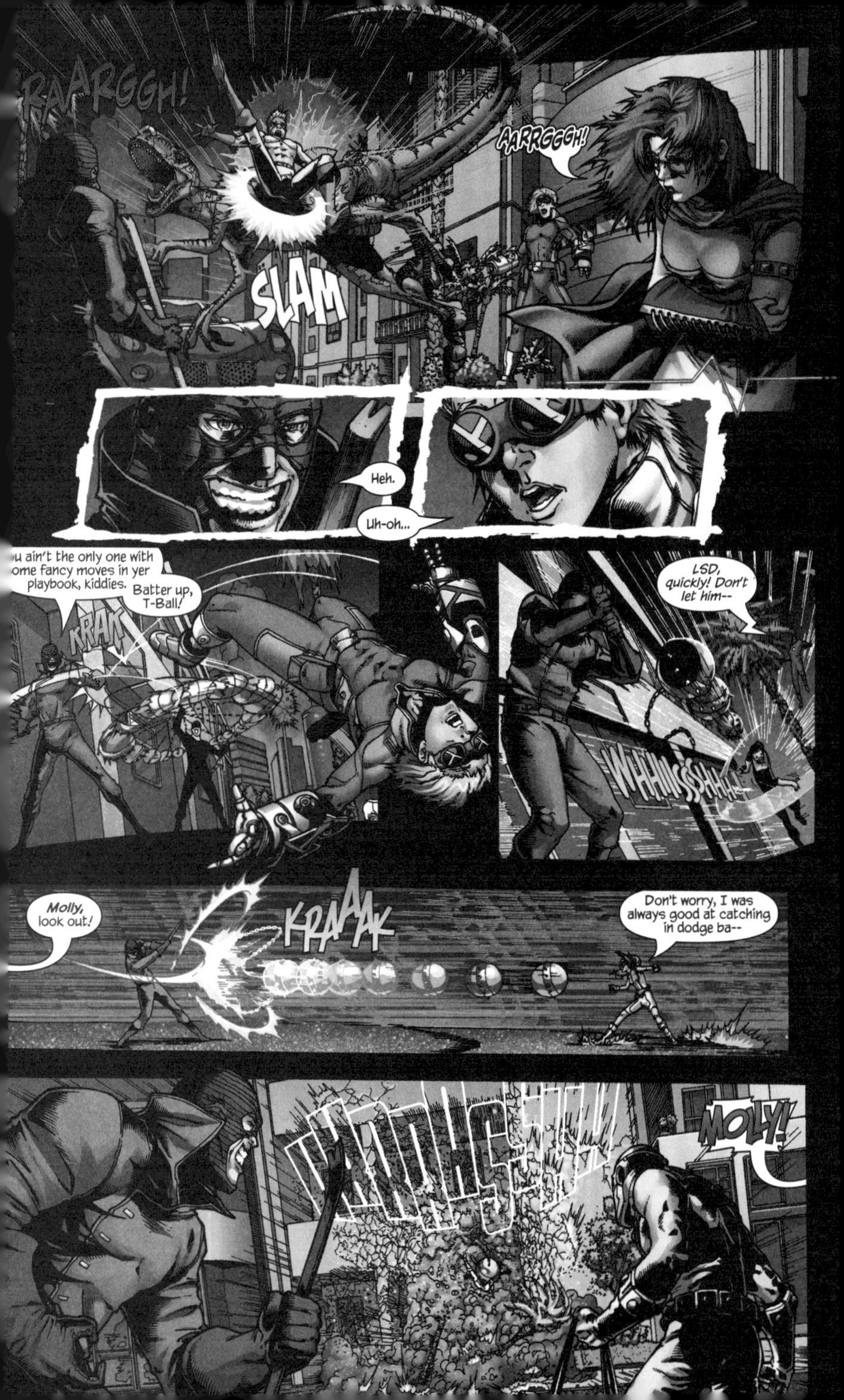

RAARGGH!
SLAM
AARRGGGH!
Heh.
Uh-oh...
ou ain't the only one with ome fancy moves in yer playbook, kiddies.
Batter up, T-Ball!
KRAK
LSD, quickly! Don't let him--
WHHHSSHHH
Molly, look out!
KRAAAAK
Don't worry, I was always good at catching in dodge ba--
MOLY!

She's stable and her vitals are good. Standing up to a blast like that...

Molly's invulnerability is much greater than I previously calculated.

I didn't mean it like that.

Then how about showing a little bedside manner by taking off your helmet?

How many times do I have to tell you--?!

"Than you calculated?!" What is she, your patient or a lab rat?

Stop it, both of you! Molly needs peace and quiet now!

We'll monitor her in shifts. I'll take the first watch. Everyone out!

Are we really doing the right thing here? I mean, what good will any of this all be if we continually get hurt... or killed?

That's the cost of being a super hero, Nico!

We all knew this going in. We can't quit now!

You know, us Runaways were doing just fine on our own till you got here, dude.

that so, e?" Care to the game o far?

Almost killed by your parents. Infiltrated by vampires. Absorbed into the Dark Dimension. Alex Wilder getting killed. Need I go on?

Yes, but now you e a chance to do more n get by, Chase. Can't you see that?!

But we got by and we survived.

Now you have a chance to save the world!

"Save the world." You're like a broken record with that.

So what's next, you wanna dress Karolina up like a cheerleader?

Let's put 'em back in your pants and cool down, gents.

I have better things to do than sit here and listen to your #$%€!

I'll be in my room. Maybe it's not too late yet to track down the Wrecking Crew...

Why do you have to needle him like that, Chase?

It's just... I'm starting to have my doubts.

And why do you constantly defend him, Gert?

Besides, it was Nico who brought it up in the first place!

You and me both, sister. I mean, we've been flying on blind faith since we met him...

...but how much do we really know about Mr. Buns-of-Steel there?

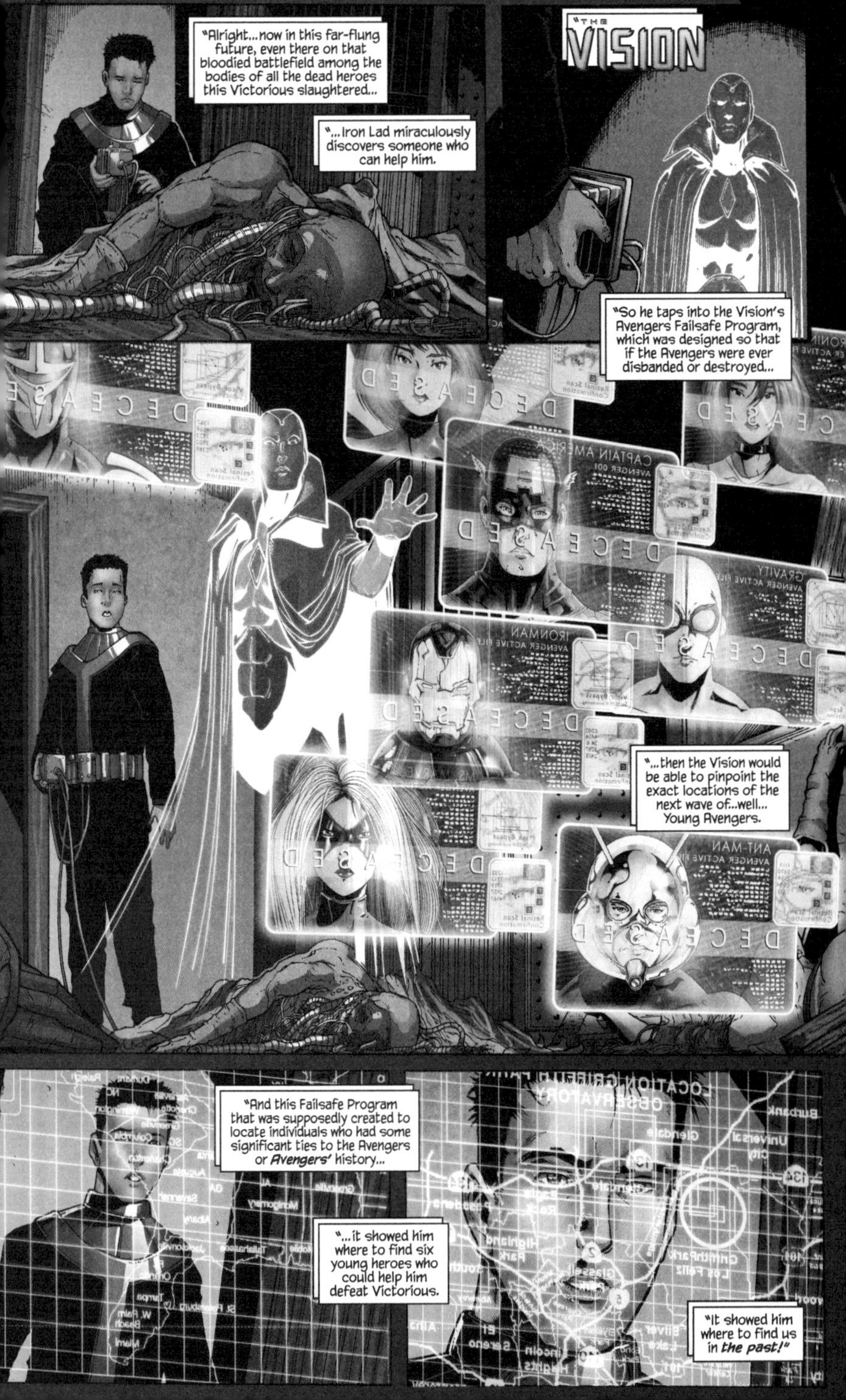
"Alright...now in this far-flung future, even there on that bloodied battlefield among the bodies of all the dead heroes this Victorious slaughtered...
"...Iron Lad miraculously discovers someone who can help him.
"THE
VISION
"So he taps into the Vision's Avengers Failsafe Program, which was designed so that if the Avengers were ever disbanded or destroyed...
CAPTAIN AMERICA
AVENGER 001
GRAVITY
AVENGER ACTIVE FILE
IRONMAN
AVENGER ACTIVE FILE
ANT-MAN
AVENGER ACTIVE FILE
DECEASED
"...then the Vision would be able to pinpoint the exact locations of the next wave of...well... Young Avengers.
"And this Failsafe Program that was supposedly created to locate individuals who had some significant ties to the Avengers or *Avengers'* history...
"...it showed him where to find six young heroes who could help him defeat Victorious.
LOCATION: GRIFFITH PARK OBSERVATORY
"It showed him where to find us in ***the past!***"

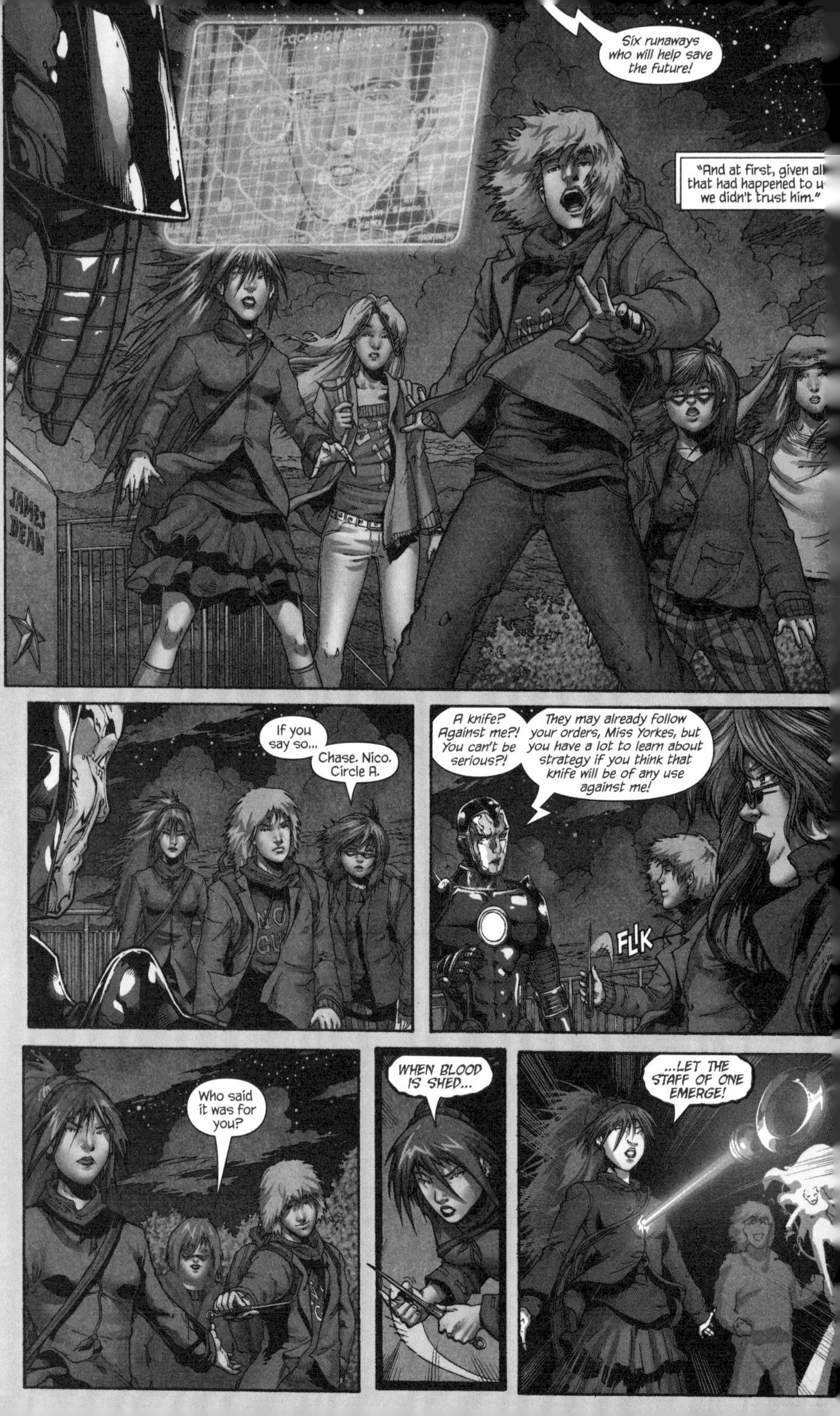
Six runaways who will help save the future!
"And at first, given all that had happened to u we didn't trust him."
JAMES DEAN
If you say so...
Chase. Nico. Circle A.
A knife? Against me?! You can't be serious?!
They may already follow your orders, Miss Yorkes, but you have a lot to learn about strategy if you think that knife will be of any use against me!
FLIK
Who said it was for you?
WHEN BLOOD IS SHED...
...LET THE STAFF OF ONE EMERGE!

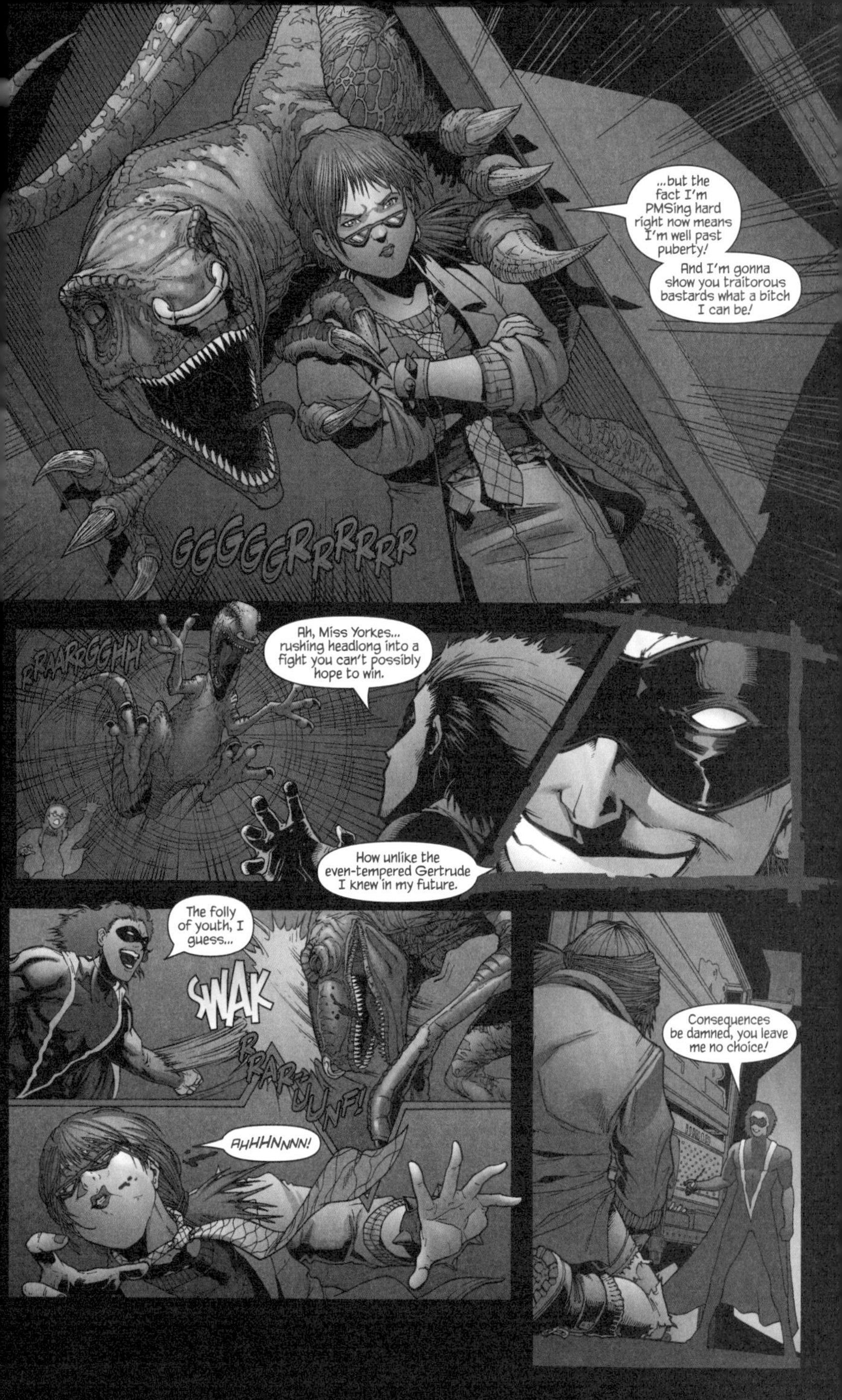

...but the fact I'm PMSing hard right now means I'm well past puberty!
And I'm gonna show you traitorous bastards what a bitch I can be!
GGGGGRRRRRR
RRAARRGGHH
Ah, Miss Yorkes... rushing headlong into a fight you can't possibly hope to win.
How unlike the even-tempered Gertrude I knew in my future.
The folly of youth, I guess...
SWAK
RRAR-UUNF!
AHHHNNNN!
Consequences be damned, you leave me no choice!

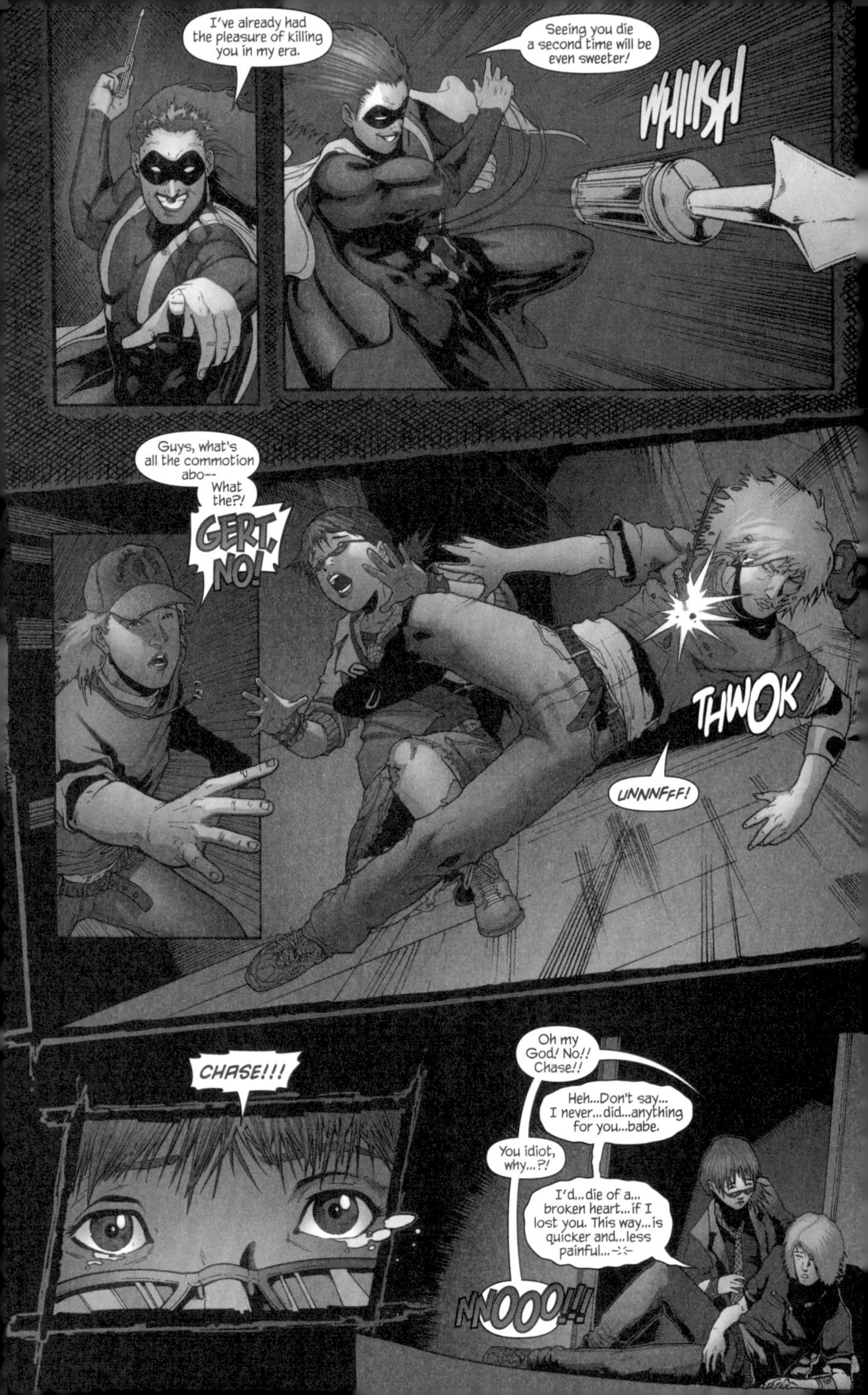

I've already had the pleasure of killing you in my era.
Seeing you die a second time will be even sweeter!
WHIIISH
Guys, what's all the commotion abo-- What the?!
GERT, NO!
THWOK
UNNNFFF!
CHASE!!!
Oh my God! No!! Chase!!
Heh...Don't say... I never...did...anything for you...babe.
You idiot, why...?!
I'd...die of a... broken heart...if I lost you. This way...is quicker and...less painful...
NNOOO!!!

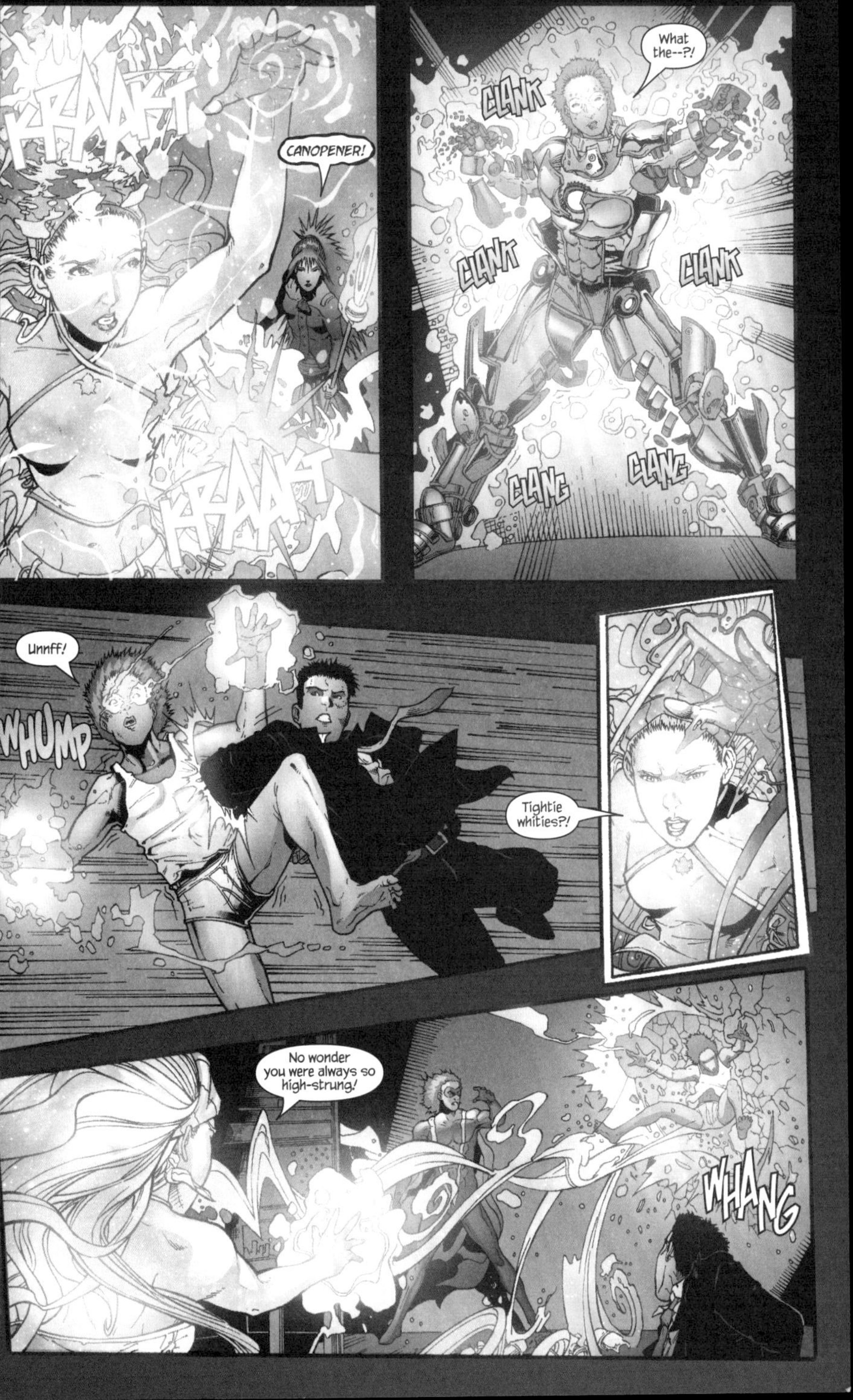
KRAAKT
CANOPENER!
KRAAKT
What the--?!
CLANK
CLANK
CLANK
CLANG
CLANG
Unnff!
WHUMP
Tightie whities?!
No wonder you were always so high-strung!
WHANG

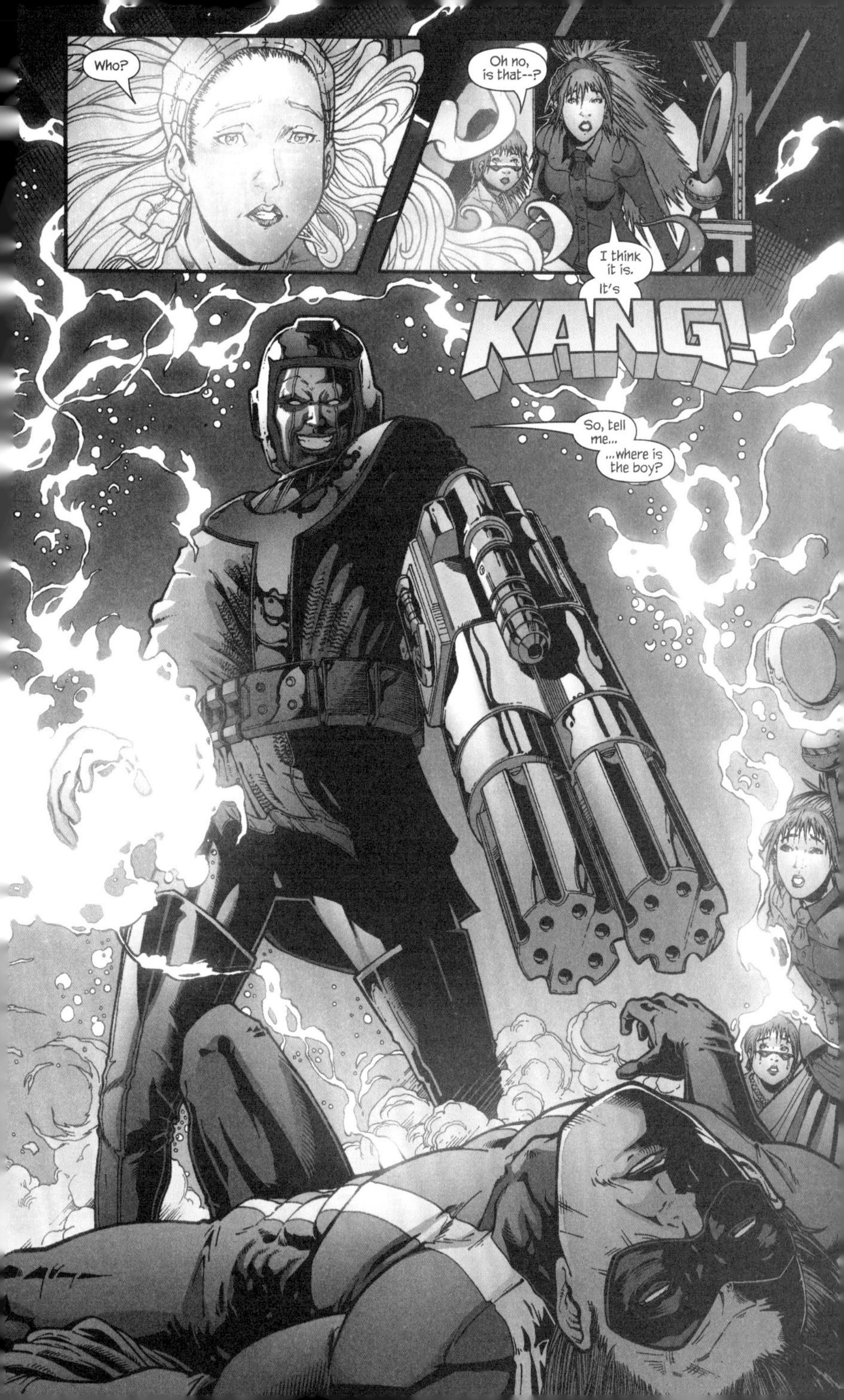
Who?
Oh no, is that--?
I think it is.
It's
KANG!
So, tell me...
...where is the boy?

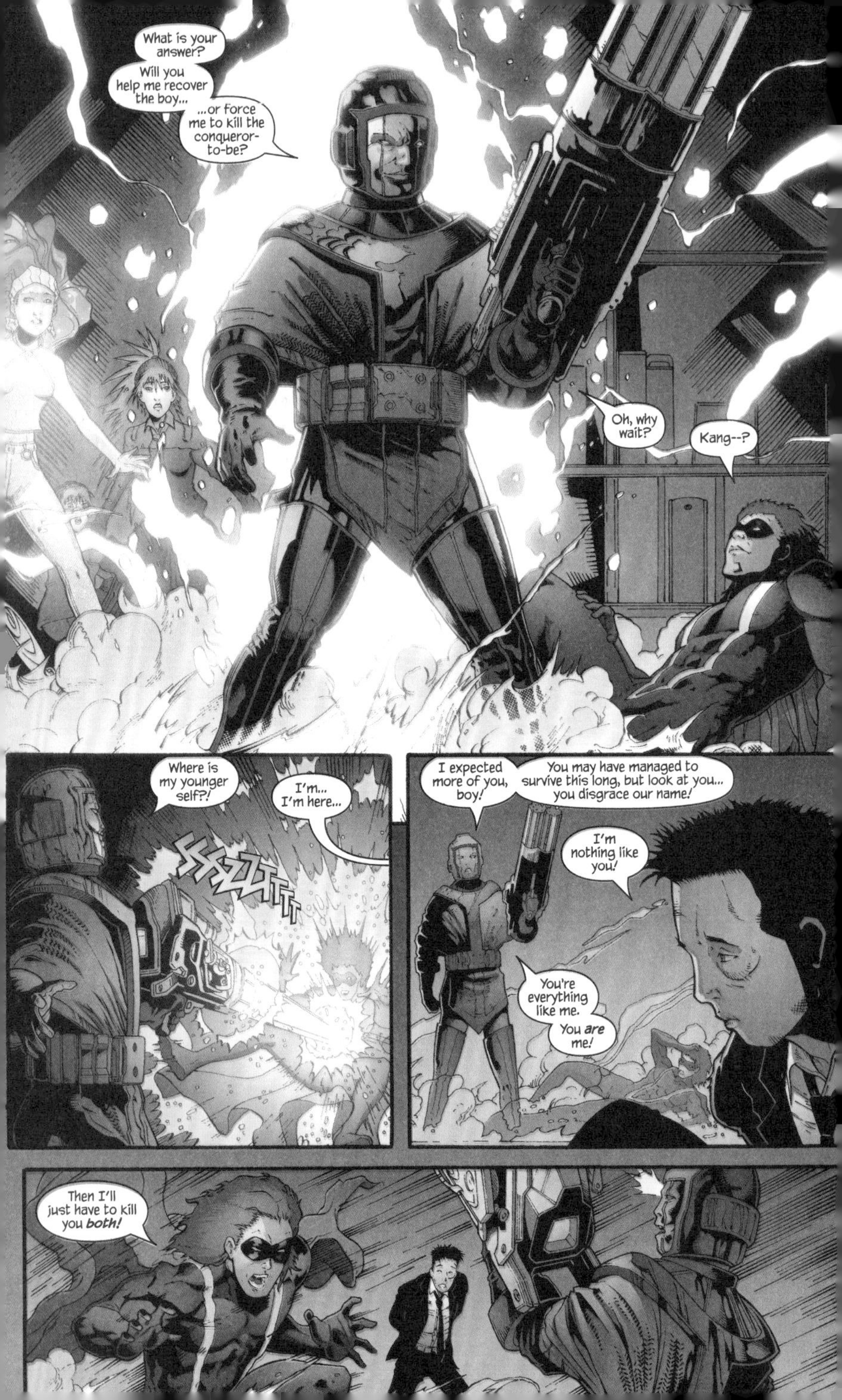
What is your answer?
Will you help me recover the boy...
...or force me to kill the conqueror-to-be?
Oh, why wait?
Kang--?
Where is my younger self?!
I'm... I'm here...
SSSZZTTTT
I expected more of you, boy!
You may have managed to survive this long, but look at you... you disgrace our name!
I'm nothing like you!
You're everything like me.
You *are* me!
Then I'll just have to kill you *both!*

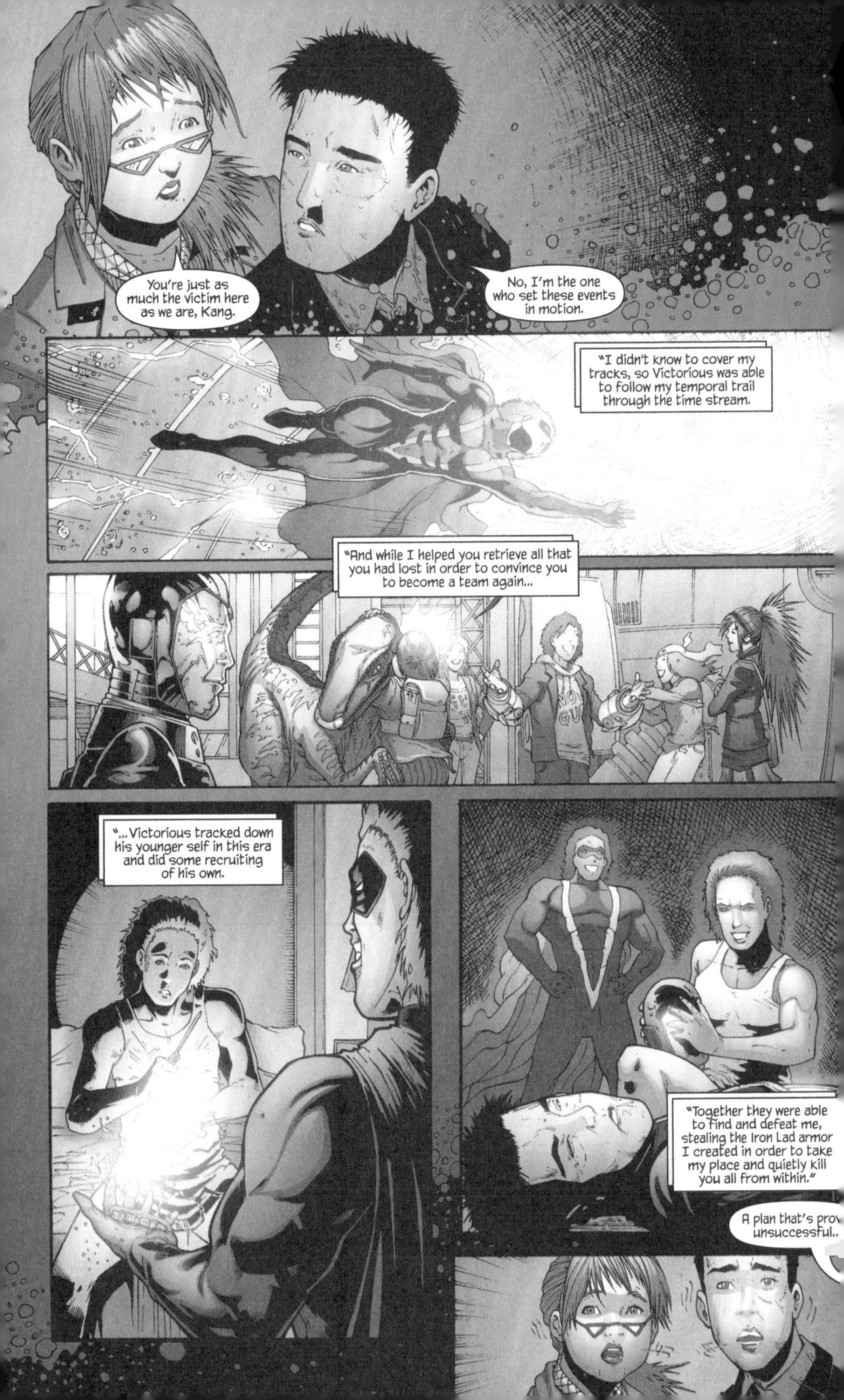
You're just as much the victim here as we are, Kang.
No, I'm the one who set these events in motion.
"I didn't know to cover my tracks, so Victorious was able to follow my temporal trail through the time stream.
"And while I helped you retrieve all that you had lost in order to convince you to become a team again...
"...Victorious tracked down his younger self in this era and did some recruiting of his own.
"Together they were able to find and defeat me, stealing the Iron Lad armor I created in order to take my place and quietly kill you all from within."
A plan that's prov unsuccessful..

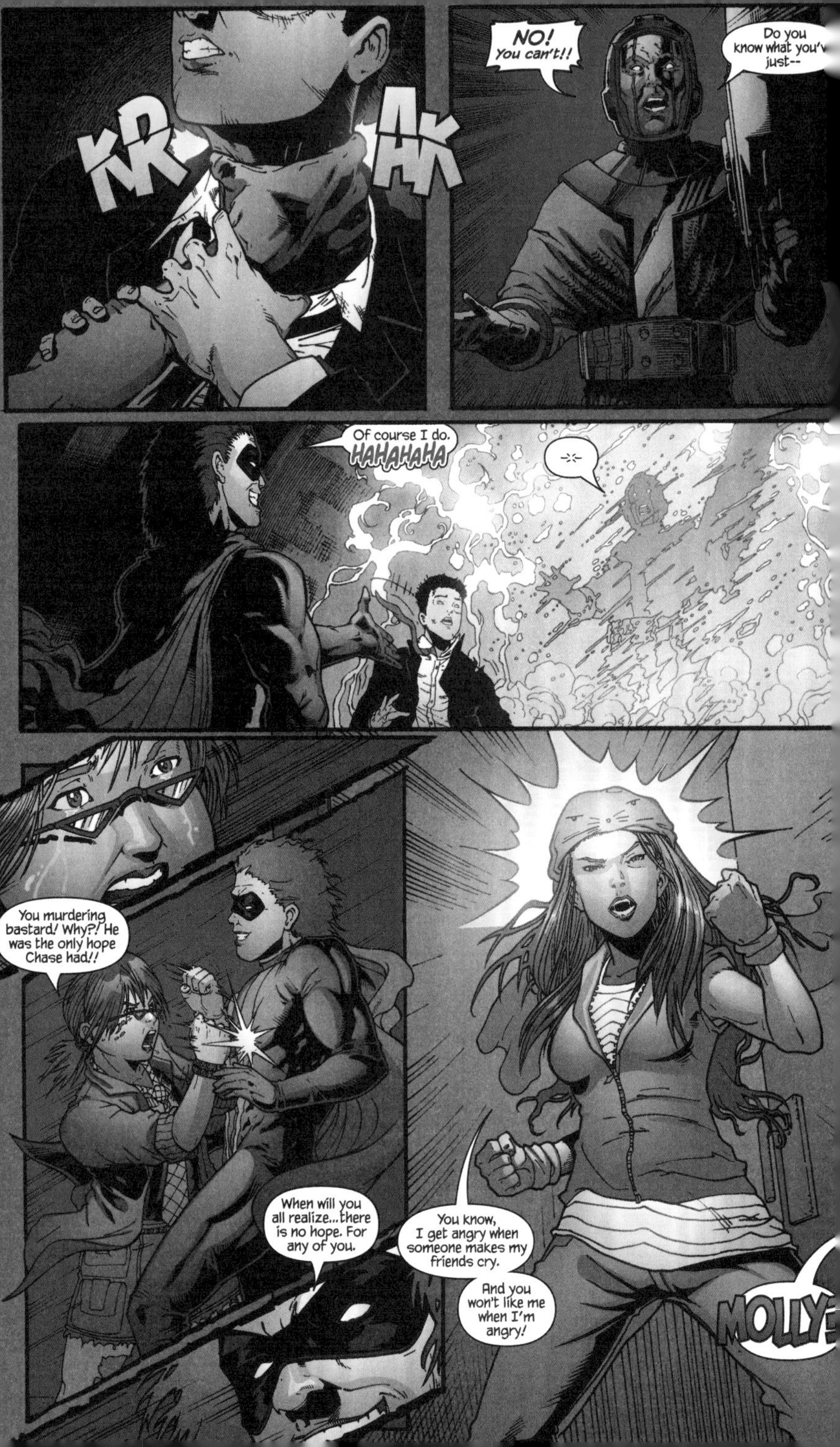
KRAK
NO! You can't!!
Do you know what you'v just--
Of course I do. HAHAHAHA
You murdering bastard! Why?! He was the only hope Chase had!!
When will you all realize...there is no hope. For any of you.
You know, I get angry when someone makes my friends cry.
And you won't like me when I'm angry!
MOLLY

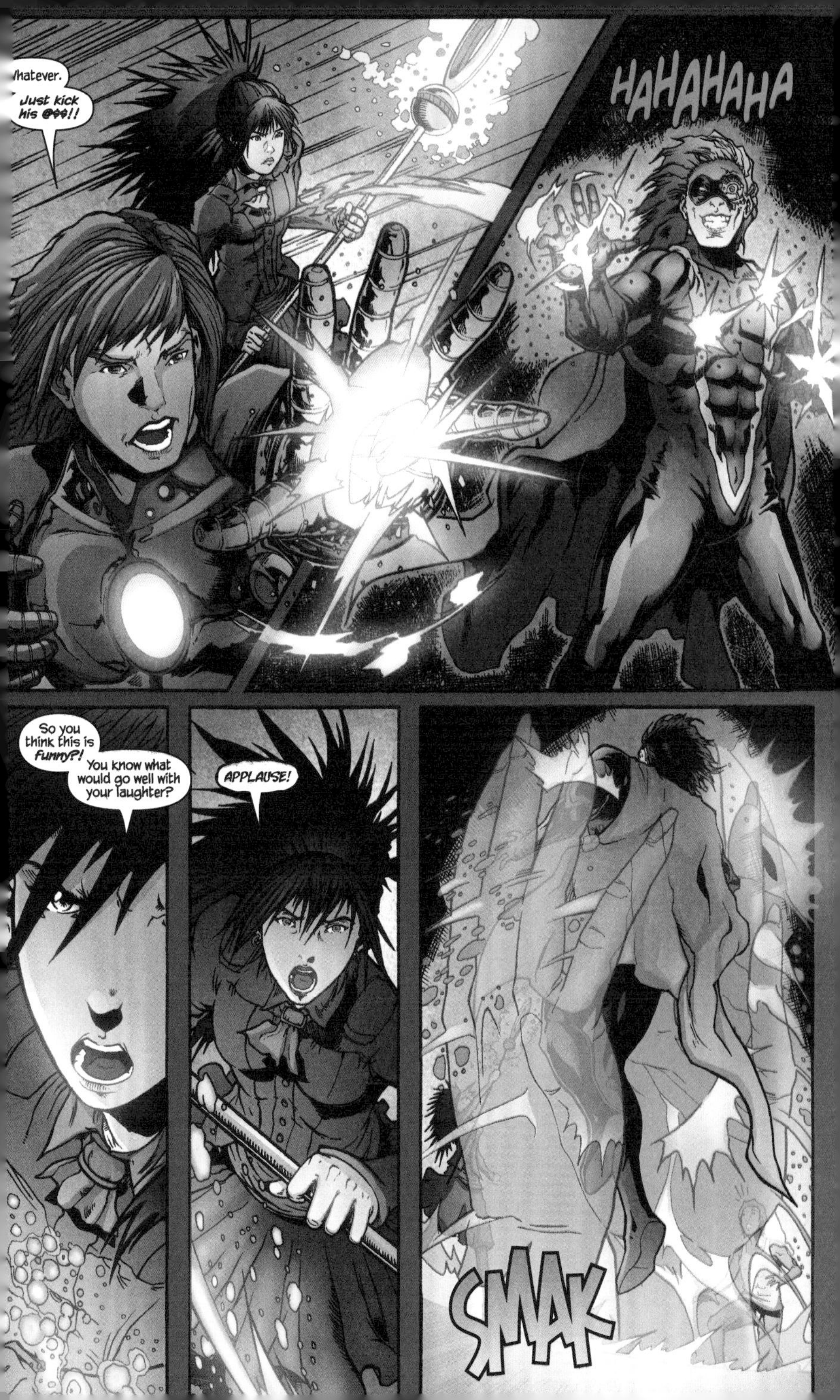
Whatever.
Just kick his @$$!!
HAHAHAHA
So you think this is funny?!
You know what would go well with your laughter?
APPLAUSE!
SMAK

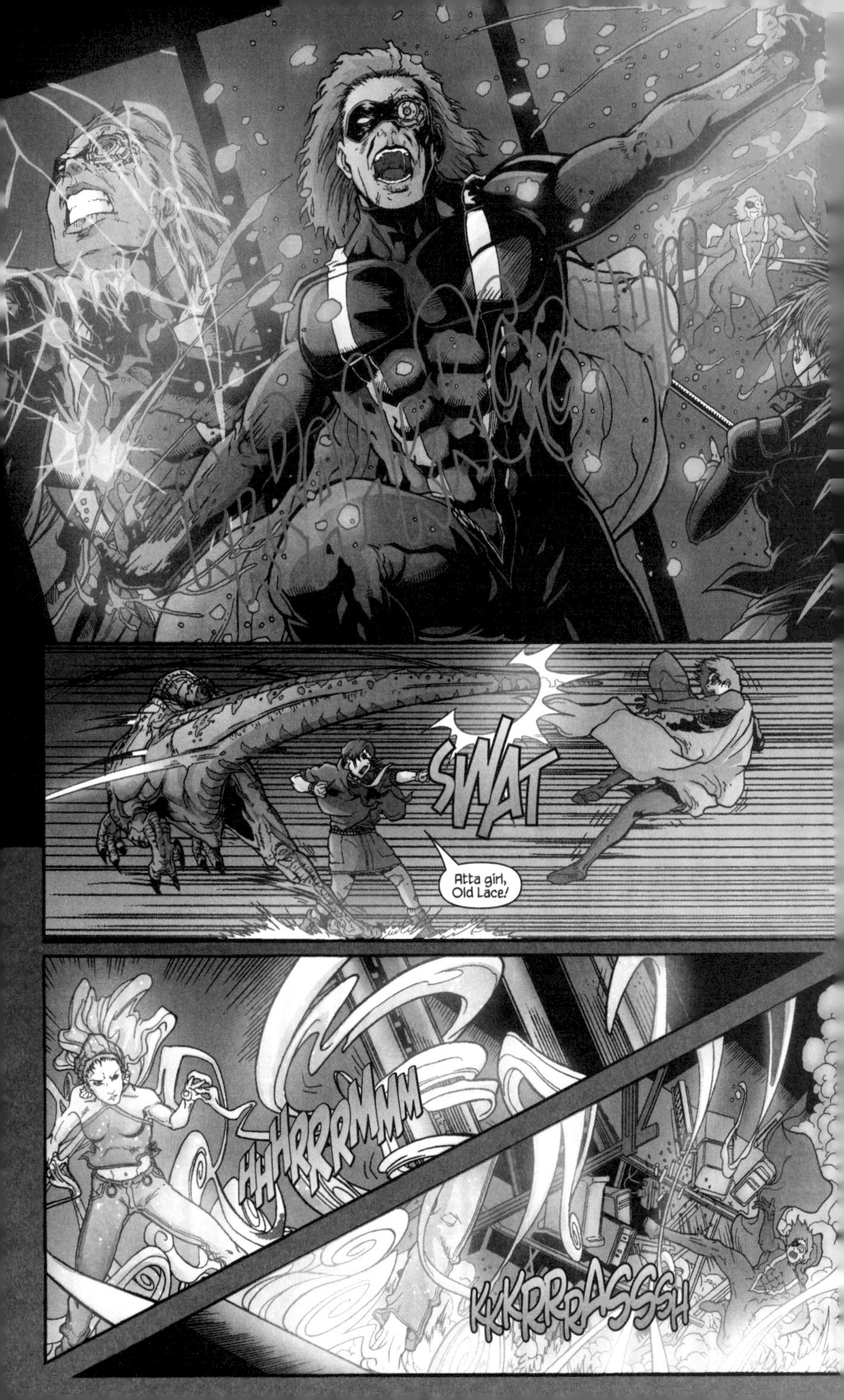
SWAT
Atta girl, Old Lace!
HHHRRRMMM
KKKRRRASSSH

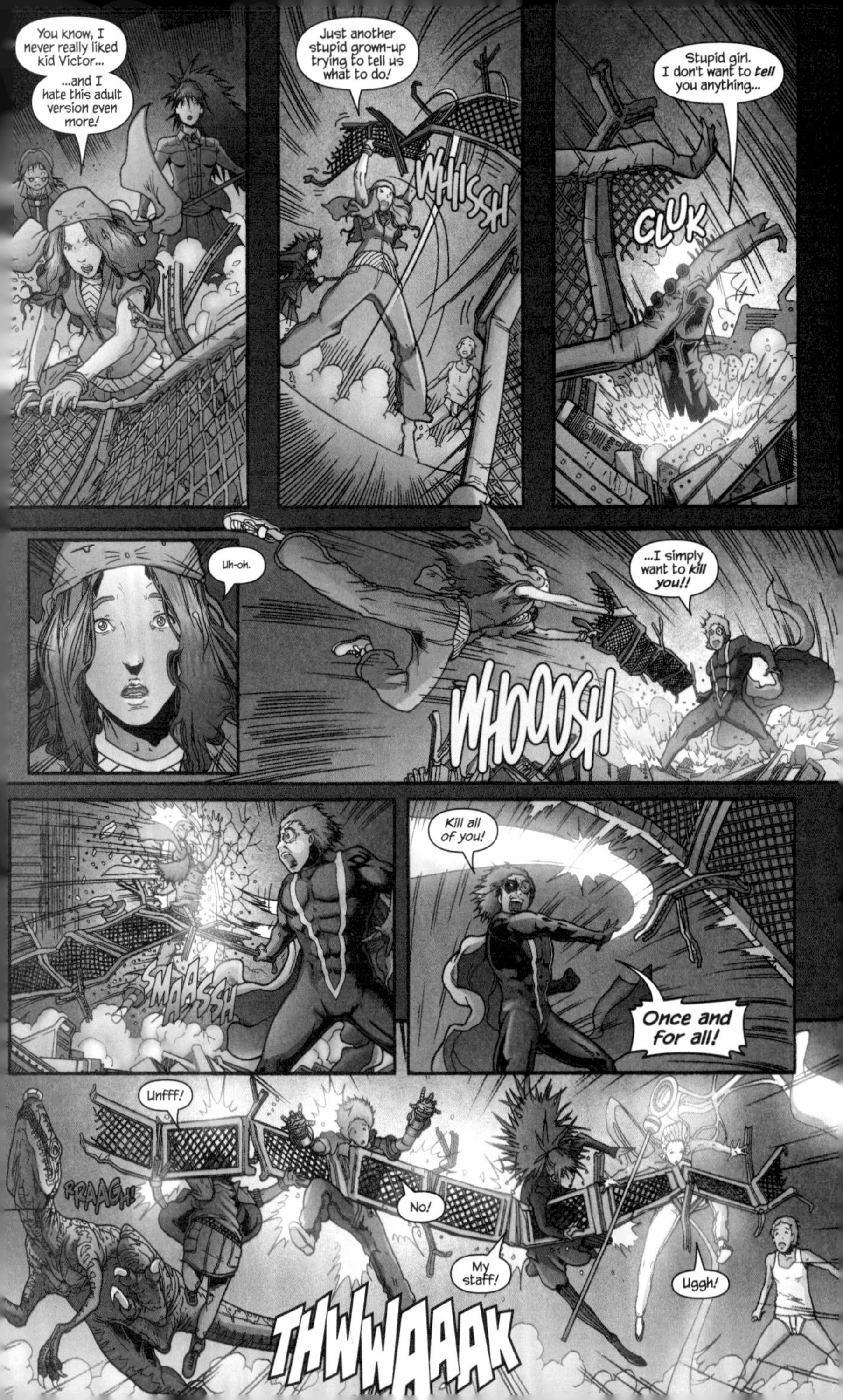
You know, I never really liked kid Victor...
...and I hate this adult version even more!
Just another stupid grown-up trying to tell us what to do!
WHISSH
Stupid girl. I don't want to *tell* you anything...
CLUK
Uh-oh.
...I simply want to *kill* you!!
WHOOOSH
SMAASSH
Kill all of you!
Once and for all!
Unfff!
RRAAGH!
No!
My staff!
Uggh!
THWWAAAK

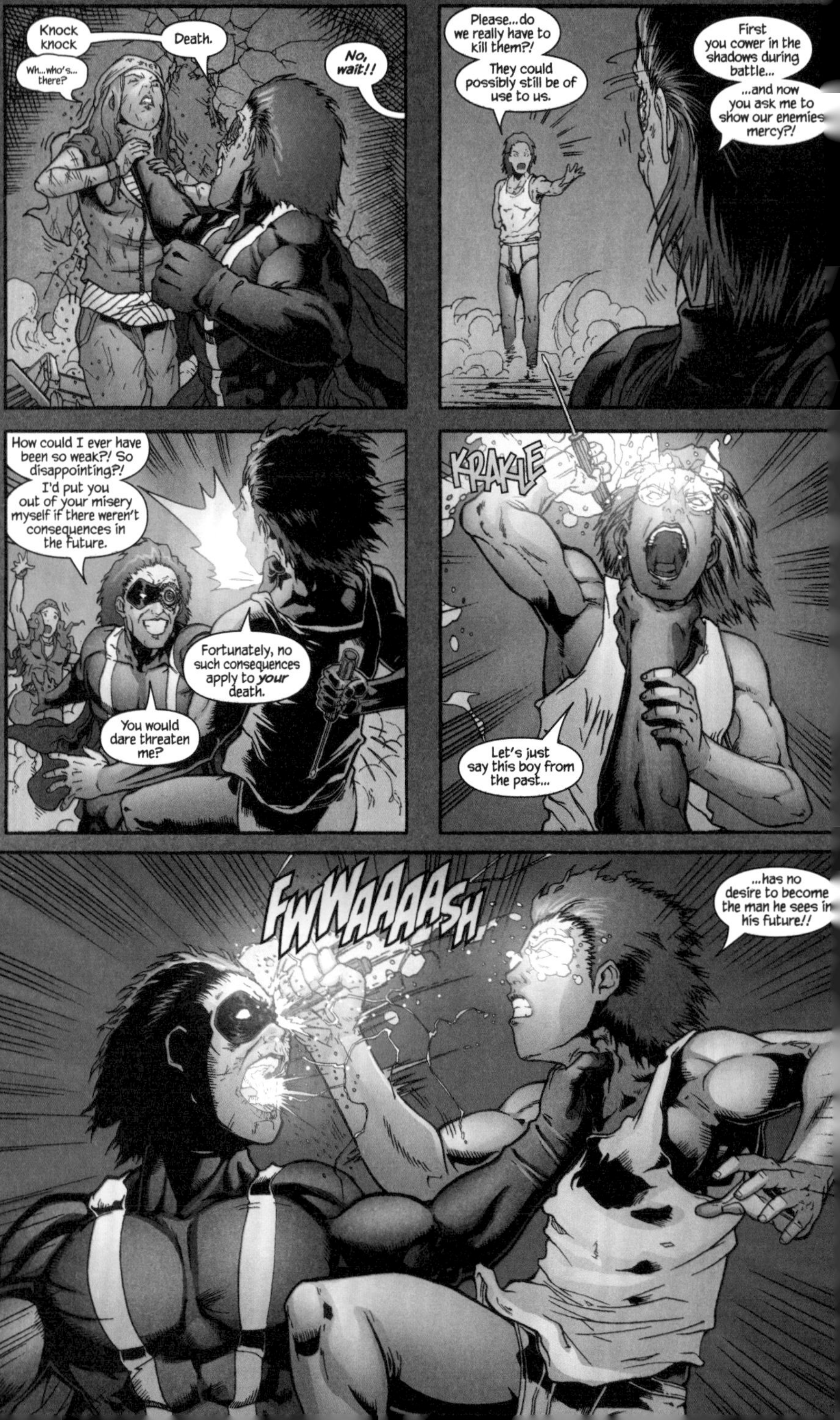
Knock knock
Wh...who's... there?
Death.
No, wait!!
Please...do we really have to kill them?!
They could possibly still be of use to us.
First you cower in the shadows during battle...
...and now you ask me to show our enemies mercy?!
How could I ever have been so weak?! So disappointing?!
I'd put you out of your misery myself if there weren't consequences in the future.
Fortunately, no such consequences apply to *your* death.
You would dare threaten me?
KRAKLE
Let's just say this boy from the past...
FWWAAAASH
...has no desire to become the man he sees in his future!!

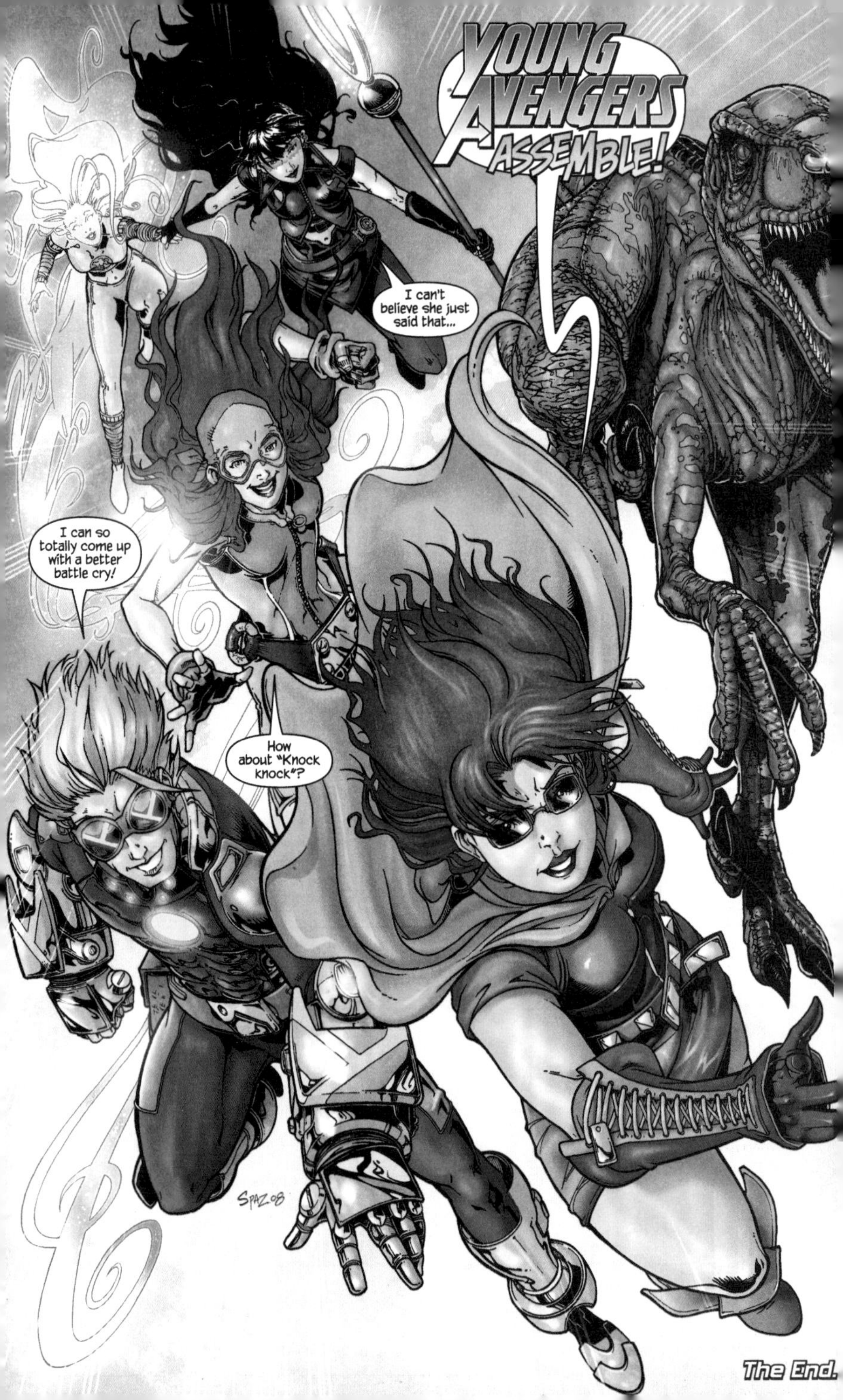
YOUNG AVENGERS ASSEMBLE!
I can't believe she just said that...
I can so totally come up with a better battle cry!
How about "Knock knock"?
SPAZ 08
The End.